TEAMTHINK

TeamThink

72 Ways to Make Good,
Smart, Quick Decisions
in Any Meeting

Ava S. Butler
Gemini Consulting

McGraw-Hill

New York   San Francisco   Washington, D.C.   Auckland   Bogotá
Caracas   Lisbon   London   Madrid   Mexico City   Milan
Montreal   New Delhi   San Juan   Singapore
Sydney   Tokyo   Toronto

Library of Congress Cataloging-in-Publication Data

Butler, Ava S.
   TeamThink : 72 ways to make good, smart, quick decisions in any
meeting / Ava S. Butler.
      p.   cm.
   Includes index.
   ISBN 0-07-009432-2 (hc : alk. paper).—ISBN 0-07-009433-0 (pbk.
: alk. paper).
    1. Business meetings. 2. Decision-making, Group. 3. Work groups.
I. Title.
   HF5734.5.B88 1996
   658.4'036—dc20   96-12071
                                         CIP

McGraw-Hill

A Division of The McGraw·Hill Companies

The sponsoring editor for this book was Betsy Brown, the editing supervisor was Fred Dahl, and the production supervisor was Suzanne W. B. Rapcavage. It was set in Frugal Sans by Inkwell Publishing Services.

Printed and bound by R. R. Donnelley & Sons Company.

McGraw-Hill books are available at special quantity discounts to use as premiums and sales promotions, or for use in corporate training programs. For more information, please write to the Director of Special Sales, McGraw-Hill, 11 West 19th Street, New York 10011. Or contact your local bookstore.

 This book is printed on recycled, acid-free paper containing a minimum of 50 percent recycled, de-inked fiber.

Contents

Introduction   ix

1 The Foundations   1

Don't You Just Love Meetings?   *1*
Why Use Participative Techniques?   *2*
Is This Book for Me?   *3*
How This Book Will Help You   *3*
How to Use This Book   *4*
Accommodating Individual Styles   *5*
Attributes of an Effective Meeting Facilitator   *6*
What About the Participants?   *8*
In Summary   *9*

2 Before the Meeting   11

Planning Your Meeting   *11*
Step One: Premeeting Planning Questions   *13*
Step Two: Creating an Agenda   *18*
Preparing the Meeting Environment   *19*
Recording the Minutes of the Meeting   *24*
More Inside Information   *24*
In Summary   *26*

3 20 Techniques to Improve Meeting Productivity 27

1 Introductions   29
2 Clearing   31
3 Ground Rules   34
4 Pulse Check   37
5 Unfinished Business   40
6 Verbal Warnings   42
7 The Bell   44
8 3P Statements   45
9 Shredded Questions   47
10 Self-Management   50
11 Go/No Go   52
12 Charting   53
13 Art   55
14 Analogies and Metaphors   57
15 Breaks   60
16 Movement   62
17 Toys   64
18 Music   66
19 Writing   68
20 Small Groups   70

4 7 Techniques to Boost Creativity and Teamwork 73

21 Thinking Out of the Box   74
22 New Glasses   76
23 Incrediballs   78
24 Team Learning   81
25 Two Truths and a Lie   83
26 Milestones   85
27 The Funeral   87

5 6 Techniques to Brainstorm Ideas 89

28 The Old-Fashioned Way   90

29 Mindmapping   *92*
30 Story Boarding   *97*
31 Card Clusters   *99*
32 STP   *102*
33 Breaking a Stalemate   *105*

6 18 Techniques to Gather Information   *107*

34 Open-Ended Questions   *108*
35 Individual Interviews   *110*
36 Focus Groups   *113*
37 Questionnaires   *116*
38 Delphi Technique   *119*
39 Expectations Survey   *121*
40 Passing Notes   *124*
41 Skits   *128*
42 Is/Is Not   *131*
43 Nominal Group Process   *133*
44 Process Flowcharting   *135*
45 Content Experts   *139*
46 Prouds and Sorries   *142*
47 Keep/Throw   *145*
48 Working Break   *147*
49 New Shoes   *149*
50 5 Whys   *151*
51 SWOTs   *152*

7 11 Techniques to Make Decisions   *157*

52 Vroom Yetton Decision-Making Model   *158*
53 Multivoting   *160*
54 Negative Voting   *162*
55 Dots   *164*
56 100 Votes   *166*
57 Nominal Prioritization   *168*
58 3 For/3 Against   *170*

59 Idea Swap *171*
60 Criteria Matrix *173*
61 Impact and Changeability Analysis *179*
62 Force Field Analysis *181*

8 7 Techniques to Implement Decisions *184*

63 Smart Goals *185*
64 Chart Actions *188*
65 Goal Plan Go *190*
66 Tree Chart *192*
67 Call for Involvement *194*
68 Test for Support *197*
69 Individual Action Planning *200*

9 3 Techniques to Evaluate Meeting Effectiveness *202*

70 What Went Well/Opportunities for Improvement *203*
71 Team Effectiveness Chart *208*
72 Written Questions *211*

Index *214*

Introduction

Over a billion meetings are held worldwide every year. Organizational experts and leading organizations predict 7 to 9 percent annual increases. That's a lot of meetings! With meetings costing organizations up to 15 percent of their personnel budgets, literally trillions of dollars are being spent on these meetings every year. To add even more dimension and focus to these awesome numbers, up to 50 percent of meeting time is wasted!

The common denominator among every one of these meetings is the meeting facilitator. Very likely, you are one of the hundreds of thousands of people who now facilitate, will facilitate, or want to facilitate meetings. You probably know that meeting facilitators are no longer limited by job title. More and more people, on every level of every organization, are being called on to facilitate meetings. This is due to the dramatic changes in how organizations communicate, delegate responsibility, and respond to their customers' needs. You could be an executive or director, a manager or supervisor, a quality improvement or reengineering specialist, a strategic planning expert, an association, community, or political leader, a human resource professional, a project leader, a team leader, or a consultant. You might work for or with a manufacturing company, a nonprofit organization, a governmental agency, a professional association, a service business, a retailer, or any organization that holds meetings.

When I began to research the feasibility of this project, I read every meeting management book I could get my hands on. I drew three conclusions. First, although nearly 20 books were available, they were of very limited practical use to contemporary meeting facilitators. Many of these books offer interesting statistical, theoretical, and anecdotal information. Others work to improve presentation skills and discuss meeting basics.

But very few of these books reflect new organizational thinking. Organizations have changed. The old organizational models, on which nearly all these meeting management books are based, have given way to a focus on organizational learning, teamwork, and participative decision making. *TeamThink* incorporates this new focus and is based on the philosophies of today's organizations. So that you will better understand these organizational and operational changes, a significant portion of Chap. 1, "The Foundations," is devoted to this subject.

Second, these books offer very few specific meeting facilitation techniques. Yet the importance of specific meeting facilitation techniques can't be overemphasized. Techniques are the tools of the trade for meeting facilitators. Imagine a carpenter with only ten tools, a plumber with only five tools, or a surgeon with only fifteen tools. *TeamThink* provides 72 state-of-the-art meeting facilitation techniques that save time, increase quality, and improve results. In fact, this book offers more specific meeting facilitation techniques alone than all the other books combined.

Third, very few of the existing books are presented in a format that makes the facilitation techniques easy to find. The techniques that are offered are usually hidden within the texts. The format of *TeamThink* is specifically designed for easy scanning and quick reference.

In summary: Among the other meeting management books currently available, few reflect the new organizational models, very few facilitation techniques are described, and those techniques tend to be cumbersome to find. That is why I have written this book. *TeamThink* provides a comprehensive set of specific, contemporary techniques that give meeting facilitators the skills they need to make today's meetings work.

In addition to the meeting basics described in Chap. 2, "Before the Meeting," this book offers the "why," "what," "when," and, most importantly, the "how" for 72 field-tested participative techniques used by the experts. These techniques, which function as meeting building blocks, or tools, are categorized by purpose. You will learn how to successfully facilitate groups to:

- Improve Meeting Productivity—Chap. 3
- Boost Creativity and Teamwork—Chap. 4
- Brainstorm Ideas—Chap. 5
- Gather Information—Chap. 6
- Make Decisions—Chap. 7
- Implement Decisions—Chap. 8
- Evaluate Meeting Effectiveness—Chap. 9

The payoffs for utilizing these techniques are profound. In addition to decreasing meeting time and cost, their application increases:

- Meeting effectiveness and efficiency.
- Creativity.
- Ownership of ideas, decisions, and plans for implementation.
- Teamwork.

- Customer satisfaction.
- Competitiveness.
- The number of happy and willing participants.

But this book doesn't contain every meeting facilitation technique. There isn't enough room in one volume for a number of specialized and advanced techniques, such as "one off" team-building techniques and techniques for defining strategy. Although most of the techniques described are supported by available computer technology, there isn't enough space in this volume to describe that technology in detail. And more and more techniques are being developed and embraced every day.

In the end, I'm just like you. I want to do my job better than ever before. And like you, I am continually looking for new ideas and processes to further improve the meetings I facilitate. I encourage you to send me your ideas about techniques that have worked for you. I will look forward to trying them myself and possibly even including them in the sequel to this book. But, for now, I trust that the techniques described in *TeamThink* will immediately and significantly improve the results of your meetings and the organizations you serve. Good luck and I look forward to your feedback.

ACKNOWLEDGMENTS

Thanks to:

- Ruth Zaslow of RZ Communications for her ideas, inspiration, focus, and hours of editing support during the early stages of the book proposal.
- Tracy Schneider, TLS Marketing, for her marketing ideas, encouragement, and enthusiasm.
- John Peterson for his logistical support.
- Michael Snell, my literary agent, for his guidance, advice, and efforts that made this book a successful prospect in the publisher's eyes.
- Betsy Brown, my editor at McGraw-Hill.
- Most of all, Richard Ping, my husband and word wizard. Without his editing support, inspiration, and insights this book would never have been possible.

Ava S. Butler

TEAMTHINK

1

The Foundations

DON'T YOU JUST LOVE MEETINGS?

Cynthia and some of her work team are eating lunch together after their weekly staff meeting. They seem depressed and tired. *"Let's face it,"* she sighs. *"Our meetings are a drag."*

"Tell me about it," shudders Ling. *"They have the ambience of a funeral."*

"And what's the point?" Cynthia adds. *"All they do is ramble on, and then there's you know who. He never stops complaining."*

"I don't even care anymore," snorts Andre between bites. *"Nothing ever happens anyway. I stopped listening months ago."*

"It's more like a war zone, if you ask me," Richard counters. *"You could cut the tension in there with a knife. Anger, bias, politics, heated debates over the littlest thing: it's like a soap opera. And if those blowhards from marketing try to push one more thing down our throats I'll go crazy."*

Frank looks up with a cynical grin. *"How about the companywide meeting last month? What a mindless, feel-good session that was. The only thing missing was group calisthenics while singing the company song over a bonfire covered with roasting marshmallows. They can take that kind of motivation and shove it."*

"It was unbelievable," Juanita agrees. *"As if anything would change as a result of that. How stupid do these managers think we are?"*

Ling laughs, *"Managers think. That's an oxymoron, isn't it?"*

"We're supposed to be cutting costs," Juanita replies. *"How much do you think those meetings cost, anyway? We waste hundreds, probably thousands of hours a year. And any idiot knows that time is money."*

"It's like the elephant in the room that nobody talks about," blasts Richard. *"Why not improve the one thing that impacts us all? Our meetings!"*

It's true. Meetings can be a real drag. Not surprisingly, meetings are perceived as the number one time waster in most organizations. To add even more suffering to the almost constant pain of these meetings, more are held now than ever before. And brace yourself, because their number will continue to grow and grow. Quality improvement, reengineering, transformation, changes in corporate policies, special customer requests, problem solving, decision making, strategy: you name it! Another meeting is created.

Meetings are where people experience and observe an organization's culture. This culture is defined and perpetuated through meetings. Is time valued or wasted? Are people's ideas encouraged and used, or dismissed? Are problems addressed proactively or swept under the carpet? Are participants expected to guard their turf or work together toward the good of all? Is open, timely communication expected or discouraged?

Like Cynthia's work team, you're probably getting depressed even thinking about the current state of your meetings. But meetings don't have to be so bad. They can be a powerful and innovative tool. Even if you facilitate meetings that are widely described as disasters, take note: You don't have to be stuck in this terrible state forever. Whether the meetings you lead are one-time affairs or regular events, there is hope. You can transform even the most boring, inefficient, and unproductive meetings. Changing your meetings not only means having happier participants. It also increases the likelihood that the teams, groups, and organization you serve will survive and even prosper in the future.

WHY USE PARTICIPATIVE TECHNIQUES?

The ways in which organizations conduct their business are changing. In fact, they are evolving at an exponential rate. Increasing global and continually more sophisticated competition are driving organizations to endlessly reevaluate and challenge the basic concepts that deliver success. Failure to do so is perilous. Now, more than ever before, survival is literally at stake.

In the past, organizations functioned autocratically. Decisions were handed down through a well-defined and segregated chain of command. Through the '50s, '60s, and even into the '70s and '80s, planning and decision making were executive exercises. Meetings reflected this culture, and were used primarily to disseminate information. People within organizations were typically utilized as "a pair of hands" to perform a fixed task. The wheels turned, and for more than half a century this system seemed to work.

To gain competitive advantage in the '90s and beyond, organizations need to make both strategic and operational decisions daily and on every level of the organization. The realities of the '90s are too complex and change too rapidly for organizations to successfully utilize the centralized, top-down management styles that worked in previous decades. Now, responsibility is widely distributed throughout organizations. Decisions are made across sectors, levels, and perspectives. These changes promote team-based communication and participation, strategic thinking on every level, and quickened movement toward measurable action.

As organizations acquire, learn from, and respond to input with increased sophistication, the need for their meetings to support these changes is steadily increasing. In fact, the primary method used to employ and integrate organizational participation is through meetings. In today's rapidly changing organizations, meetings tap the power of participation! The question today is not "whether" to use participative techniques, but "how"!

IS THIS BOOK FOR ME?

If you can relate to any of the conditions on the following checklist, this book will help you to profoundly increase the efficiency, productivity, and effectiveness of the meetings that you lead or facilitate.

_____ Meeting participants yawn and sleep in our meetings.

_____ Participants don't speak up in the meetings, but talk amongst themselves afterwards.

_____ Things take longer than we want and we often run out of time.

_____ There is not enough input from some people and too much from a few.

_____ People say "I told you so" a lot in our department.

_____ Our team is under scrutiny to be more effective.

_____ New competition is forcing us to re-think our business.

_____ Our group seems stuck in a rut.

_____ Participants find every excuse under the sun not to attend our meetings.

_____ We have a new group forming and want to get off on the right track.

_____ Our meetings do not produce the results we need.

_____ We want to be world-class competitors.

_____ I wish we could accomplish more in less meeting time.

_____ I'm asked to facilitate a lot of meetings and I want to do a better job.

_____ I have an idea of *what* I need to do in order to improve our meetings. I just don't know *how* to do it.

HOW THIS BOOK WILL HELP YOU

All meetings are held to accomplish something, to obtain some result. The meeting is a means to an end. The effectiveness of a meeting has a direct impact on the quality of its intended results.

TeamThink provides the tools required to build the relevant and necessary structure for any type of meeting, and is designed to:

- serve as a quick reference for selecting the most appropriate techniques to use in the meetings you lead or facilitate, and
- provide step-by-step instructions for how to apply and use these techniques.

This book is like a working carpenter's tool box on one hand, and a master chef's cookbook on the other. It gives you all the specific tools you need to effectively deal with diverse meeting situations. It not only provides the basic hammer, nails, and hand saw, but also the more sophisticated specialty tools required to complete most any potential project. At the same time, the techniques serve as the ingredients necessary to accomplish complex tasks. Just as the recipe for perfect lasagna calls for layers of ingredients to be used one after another, meeting facilitation techniques build on each other to create the perfect agenda.

The various techniques described in *TeamThink* are designed to be used in all types of meetings, and provide meeting facilitators and their participants the capability to efficiently:

- Improve Meeting Productivity
- Boost Creativity and Teamwork
- Brainstorm Ideas
- Gather Information

- Make Decisions
- Implement Decisions
- Evaluate Meeting Effectiveness

Knowledge of the specific facilitation techniques described in this book will give you a greater depth and understanding of meeting processes. It will also increase your personal confidence and better equip you to improvise with clarity.

HOW TO USE THIS BOOK

Skim through the book
Look for what you know and what you need to know. There may be techniques which are familiar to you, or that you have used in a slightly different way. Concentrate on the parts that are most pertinent to you and the meetings you are currently planning. The novice facilitator may read the book from cover to cover, and refer to techniques again and again when planning specific meetings. The more experienced reader will likely focus on new ideas and more complex techniques.

Think of this book as your "tool box"
Every experienced facilitator has a well-developed "tool box" of specific meeting techniques to use in given situations. The variations, combinations, and adaptations of these processes are almost endless. This book is designed to provide you with essential tools for your "tool box." As you prepare for each meeting, use this book as a reference to help you accomplish your goals.

Develop and customize your own techniques
As chefs continue to learn new recipes and customize standard recipes for their own tastes, continually develop and customize techniques to meet your own style and the evolutionary needs of your organization or clients. You may find that a technique described in one section can be modified or copied to meet another ob-

jective. Be creative. A chef also knows that there is more to a meal than one course. Challenge yourself to learn how to make the techniques blend to make a perfect meeting.

Pick up ideas wherever you can. The more options you can create, the better facilitator you will become.

I encourage you to write to me with new meeting techniques. I will add as many as space allows to later editions of this book and will look forward to the opportunity to try them myself.

ACCOMMODATING INDIVIDUAL STYLES

Felix is an accountant for a small regional hospital. *"I'm a smart person, but every time I attend a meeting I feel like a fish out of water. I'm always out of sync. I used to think that I was just stupid or something, but recently I realized that the meetings were the problem. Our meetings are stuck in the decades when you were punished for writing with your left hand."*

People don't all think, learn, or interact in the same ways. The ways in which people think impact the information they communicate. Therefore, for meetings to be efficient and successful, the effective meeting facilitator must utilize techniques that reinforce and tap these different personal styles.

Some people need significant time to think before they are ready to share their ideas publicly. Others want to "talk it out," using verbal language as a method to form their thoughts. Still others prefer to share their ideas through writing. A large number of people understand an idea better with visual aids; they have to "see it." Others are tactile or "hands on" learners. Some people feel comfortable making quick decisions, and others don't.

There are seven different personal styles that exist within every person. They include musical, visual-spatial, interpersonal, intrapersonal, mathematical-logical, bodily-physical (kinesthetic), and linguistic. Naturally, each of us excels in a few of these areas. It is not surprising that the linguistic style is the one used almost exclusively in meetings. But the key to a successful meeting is to use techniques that appeal to a wider range of personal styles and aptitudes. Not only will your meetings be more interesting, they will also be far more effective. And capitalizing on these different learning styles is easier than you may think. Each of the techniques in this book is designed to incorporate one or more of these individual styles. Here are some examples.

VISUAL-SPATIAL

- Use visual aids, diagrams, charts, and illustrations. (See CHARTING, Technique 12; MINDMAPPING, Technique 29; PROCESS FLOWCHARTING, Technique 44; DOTS, Technique 55; FORCE FIELD ANALYSIS, Technique 62; and TEAM EFFECTIVENESS CHART, Technique 71.)
- Ask participants to draw their perspectives. (See ART, Technique 13.)

MUSICAL

- Use appropriate music before the meeting, during breaks, after the meeting, and as a review technique. (See MUSIC, Technique 18.)

INTERPERSONAL (RELATIONSHIPS BETWEEN PEOPLE)

- Allow people to talk amongst themselves in small groups. (See SMALL GROUPS, Technique 20.)
- Use quick exercises to allow people to know each other better. (See INTRODUCTIONS, Technique 1.)

INTRAPERSONAL (RELATIONSHIP OF PERSON WITH HIMSELF OR HERSELF)

- Allow quiet time for thinking. Write down ideas independently and silently. (See WRITING, Technique 19.)
- Ask reflective questions. (See SHREDDED QUESTIONS, Technique 9; and OPEN-ENDED QUESTIONS, Technique 34.)
- Set personal goals. (See INDIVIDUAL ACTION PLANNING, Technique 69.)

BODILY-PHYSICAL (KINESTHETIC)

- Write ideas on cards and move them into appropriate categories. (See CARD CLUSTERS, Technique 31.)
- Create movement during your meeting. (See MOVEMENT, Technique 16.)

LINGUISTIC

- Lead focused group discussions. (See CONTENT EXPERTS, Technique 45; and SWOTS, Technique 51.)
- Use analogies and metaphors. (See ANALOGIES AND METAPHORS, Technique 14.)

MATHEMATICAL-LOGICAL

- List key points in sequence. (See STORY BOARDING, Technique 30.)
- Prioritize choices and concerns. (See EXPECTATIONS SURVEY, Technique 39; MULTI-VOTING, Technique 53; 100 VOTES, Technique 56; and NOMINAL PRIORITIZATION, Technique 57.)
- Analyze issues or choices, step by step. (See CRITERIA MATRIX, Technique 60; and FORCE FIELD ANALYSIS, Technique 62.)
- Compare and contrast issues. (See IMPACT AND CHANGEABILITY ANALYSIS, Technique 61.)
- Use flow charts. (See PROCESS FLOWCHARTING, Technique 44.)

ATTRIBUTES OF AN EFFECTIVE MEETING FACILITATOR

No meeting is effective without an effective meeting facilitator. Meeting facilitation is a skill and skills can be learned. The techniques described in the following chapters are designed to enhance your skills as a facilitator. But the exceptional facilitators go beyond technical skill in creating an atmosphere of success. The relationship these people create with a group is far less tangible, but is easy to see, hear, and feel.

With few exceptions, personal attributes cannot be taught. A strong skill base can help create a foundation for these attributes to flower, but the rest is up to the individual. Following is a list of the attributes that support effective meeting facilitators. As you read them, you'll notice that they are interrelated, building on and supporting each other.

■ Good sense of humor

Humor can break the ice, cut the tension, and revive your group in even the most demanding situations. There will be times in your meetings when something less than ideal will happen, and you as the facilitator will need to handle the resulting stress with confidence, style, and grace. If you can't laugh at yourself and laugh in difficult situations, you will find meeting facilitation very trying indeed.

■ Assertiveness

As the facilitator, you need to have the ability and the guts to speak the hard truth when necessary. If you are afraid to say what needs to be said when it needs to be said, you won't be as effective or credible.

However, the challenge of assertiveness is knowing when to push and when to pull back. You need to know when to step in to keep the group on track, and when to let things work themselves out on their own. And remember, there is a big difference between assertiveness and aggressiveness.

■ Intuition

Meeting facilitation is not a skill that rests on applying a simple formula to arrive at the "right answer." You must find it on your own by identifying what is best for each situation. One could argue that intuition comes from experience, and I agree. But it also includes the ability to act on a hunch.

■ Creativity

You will need to put together techniques in new and creative ways every time you facilitate a meeting. This is true for a group meeting for the first time or for the two hundredth time. Agendas are created by pulling theories, experiences, and ideas from every direction you know and some that you don't.

■ Flexibility

The meeting facilitator who is wed to his or her first idea, or to his or her ideas in general, is going to encounter trouble. You must think on your feet, stay on your feet, accept new and better ideas from others, and change or modify course as required.

■ Confidence and enthusiasm

Without facilitator confidence and enthusiasm, a group quickly prepares for a boring, unproductive experience. The ability to appear articulate and knowledgeable in front of a group of people is essential in creating a positive atmosphere from the start.

■ Team player

If you want to be in the limelight, meeting facilitation is not the job for you. You are the moderator, the interpreter, and the timekeeper, but not the star. Your recognition comes from the work you allow others to accomplish and the success you help build in the organizations you serve.

Many groups alternate facilitators. This is an excellent method for building a broad base of skill and commitment across the team.

■ High self-esteem

If the meeting is not going well, the facilitator is the most likely participant to be targeted as the cause. Sometimes this is justified, sometimes not. Regardless, when a group or individual takes their frustration out on you, you can't take it personally. You must be able to separate your skill, your experiences, and your job from your worth as a human being.

■ Sincerity

Sincerity, according to my thesaurus, is the opposite of hypocrisy. You, as the facilitator, must truly care about your group and its success. You need to "walk the walk" and "practice what you preach."

■ Dedicated to learning

Good meeting facilitators are dedicated to continuously building their skills. The more tools you have available to you, the less likely you will be to panic when a certain technique doesn't work the way you planned.

WHAT ABOUT THE PARTICIPANTS?

It's great if I possess all of these wonderful attributes, but don't meeting participants have a responsibility, too? I mean, shouldn't successful meeting participants have certain attributes as well?

You're right. Meeting success is a team responsibility. The same attributes that apply to meeting facilitators apply to meeting participants. It would be fantastic if every meeting participant you came in contact with had the same attributes that make you a great facilitator. But it's not a perfect world and you are going to have to deal with all types of people in all types of situations. The full spectrum of people will populate your meetings just as they populate the earth.

It's your responsibility as a meeting facilitator to apply your experience and skill in such a way as to maximize the outcome of every meeting you lead. You will have difficult participants. You will have problems. It's never easy to make meetings work. But if you apply the techniques described in this book, 99 percent of the behavioral problems so common to meetings will never happen. The techniques take care of the problems before they occur. These techniques not only work, they are specifically designed to bring out the best in people, all people! And with the skills that this book places at your fingertips, it may even look like a piece of cake.

IN SUMMARY

The unparalleled speed of organizational change has, by necessity, placed a priority on utilizing the full potential of human resources. This has resulted in a dedication to participation and teamwork, which exposes the need for continually evolving and efficient communication. Because meetings are the venues where this communication takes place, effective meeting facilitators have become essential links in the chain of people who are responsible for organizational success.

Many people think of meetings as time wasters, with good reason. Meetings can be boring, angry, mindless, and profoundly ineffective. But their number is growing with no end in sight. There is general agreement that meetings are important in concept but not always productive. Meetings provide occasions for decisions to be made, priorities set, and changes agreed upon. They define and perpetuate organizational culture, and reveal an organization's position relative to the overall revolution now under way. If your meetings aren't changing, it's likely that your company is slow to change as well.

Meeting facilitators create the agendas and techniques which formulate meeting structure. This allows meeting participants to focus on the content of their discussions and leave the structure and processes of those conversations to the facilitator. The facilitator's job is not to define the content or outcome of any meeting. It is instead to define the structure, processes, and techniques required so that the participants can effectively accomplish the goals on their agendas.

Successful meeting facilitators possess certain attributes. They are self-confident, flexible, and have a good sense of humor. They are enthusiastic and sincere. They are assertive, creative, and intuitive. They work well with teams and are dedicated to learning. These attributes are, at best, difficult to teach.

But meeting facilitators also possess the expertise to successfully facilitate a participative meeting. This expertise arises in the form of specific skills, which are accessible to almost anybody with the will to learn. The quest for new and more effective techniques is a never-ending process. New levels of skill and knowledge are required for even the most experienced meeting facilitator. The skills of meeting facilitation are exemplified in the specific techniques described in this book. When assimilated, used, perfected, and expanded upon, they will become part of an indispensable set of tools to make meetings work, as well as to position you on the cutting edge of change.

2
Before the Meeting

Chapter 1 describes the philosophies of participation and teamwork, the fundamentals of personal learning styles, and the distinctive attributes of an accomplished meeting facilitator. These fundamentals, when coupled with effective premeeting planning and use of the specific facilitation techniques contained in this book, will lead you to become a more competent meeting leader. This chapter extends the concepts from Chap. 1 into practical advice that will help you prepare for the actual meetings you will facilitate. I will outline specific meeting components and provide an efficient and flexible template that you can use for planning all your meetings. This template includes sections that will describe how to:

- Skillfully plan your meetings
- Build concise and flexible meeting agendas
- Best prepare the physical meeting environment
- Efficiently report meeting content and results

This step-by-step, component approach simplifies the meeting process by providing the essential checklists and questions you will need answered in order to build your meetings.

PLANNING YOUR MEETING

What you do before your meetings is every bit as important as what you do during them. In fact, without effective premeeting planning and organization, the quality of your meetings will certainly suffer and some will very likely even fail. Most facilitators plan to some degree, and many consider their meetings planned if they create an agenda, send it out, book a room, and order the coffee. But proficient premeeting planning goes beyond these basics. The level of planning a facilitator attains before the meeting separates the true professional from the rank amateur. And meeting results speak for themselves. Detailed planning is essential for consistent success. But proceed with care, because as the old saying goes, "The devil is in the details."

Let's use Sam's meeting as an example. Sam has facilitated a number of meetings and he thought his meeting was well prepared. He had clarified its purpose, prepared an agenda, and the time and place were set. Figure 2-1 illustrates Sam's meeting agenda.

The goal of Sam's group was to prepare a management presentation asking for approval to purchase new equipment. He had sent out an agenda, assembled the right people, and estimated a three-hour time frame. He purposely started his meeting at 2:00 PM, which allowed the group an additional half hour if the meeting happened to take more time (quitting time was at 5:30 PM).

It sounds simple enough, doesn't it? Unfortunately, it wasn't. The meeting started off well enough. Everyone took the data they had individually collected and converted the numbers into statistics that would support their case. When they started to share this information they discovered that the numbers didn't fit together very well. The material, when integrated, just didn't create a compelling picture. To make matters worse, even though they had made some progress three and a half hours into the meeting that was scheduled for three hours, they began to question their original assumptions. The group was frustrated and angry when the meeting finished at 7:30 PM, five and a half hours after it began. And the group had spent so much time preparing the numbers that they left no time at all to practice their actual presentation. The next morning their presentation didn't flow well at all. They were asked several questions that they were ill-prepared to answer. The group's proposal for funding was ultimately turned down.

What went wrong? How could the group's efforts have been more successful? Obviously their meeting didn't adequately prepare them for their presentation,

---

MEETING AGENDA

GOAL: Prepare a management presentation asking for approval of new equipment.

TO: Jacob French, Nancy Bartlett, Anna Saiano, Andre Washington, Philip Nugent, Kim Preston, Clinton Williams, Allan Cluquot

FROM: Sam Ballard

DATE: February 5, 1996

TIME: 2:00 - 5:00 PM

PLACE: Conference Room B

Agenda	Time
1. Compile statistical data	60 minutes
2. Prepare a presentation to management	120 minutes

Figure 2-1. Sam's original meeting agenda.

which was the purpose and goal of the meeting. Their case for new equipment was a good one, but you couldn't tell that from the presentation they gave. What could they have done differently? How could the participants have best accomplished the goals of their meeting? What was the most efficient way to analyze the data? How should the group have organized themselves? Should they have analyzed the raw data first or determined up front what would most concern their customer (in this case, management)? Should they have listed all the data and agreed on their assumptions about how the numbers would be used before beginning any analysis? Did having this meeting the afternoon before the actual presentation was scheduled give them enough time? As Sam and his group found out, if this level of detail is not effectively exposed and analyzed before the meeting, the time spent in the meeting itself will likely be excessive and the results unsatisfactory.

If Sam had the opportunity to prepare for his meeting again, he would be well-served to plan it to the next level of detail. Figure 2-2 shows an enhanced agenda that would have supported Sam better in accomplishing his goals. Even though Sam's group would only have been given the outline of this agenda, this facilitator's version shows the level of detail that is necessary to lead successful meetings. Note the differences in comparison to his original agenda (Fig. 2-1).

STEP ONE: PREMEETING PLANNING QUESTIONS

This section is designed to help you avoid the premeeting planning mistakes that Sam and many other meeting facilitators typically make. Use the following Premeeting Planning Questions to support you in preparing for every meeting you facilitate. These questions cover each of the major meeting components, and will help you focus, prioritize, and reinforce your understanding of each issue. This checklist asks all the questions necessary for you to build your meeting agendas, and will tune you in to your meetings like never before.

THE CORNERSTONE QUESTIONS
- What is (are) the goal(s) of this meeting?
- Is a meeting the best way to accomplish this (these) goal(s)?
- Who should be involved in planning this meeting?
  Including key participants in planning your meetings provides better and more complete information, and pays profound dividends in the meeting itself. It allows you to discover danger spots, problems, or any potential conflicts, as well as gain insights into better ways to accomplish tasks. It creates shared ownership over meeting goals and ultimately improves the likelihood of meeting success. This collaboration is especially critical in long meetings with large groups of people and meetings of special importance.

MEETING AGENDA

GOAL: Prepare a management presentation asking for approval of new equipment.

TO: Jacob French, Nancy Bartlett, Anna Saiano, Andre Washington, Philip Nugent, Kim Preston, Clinton Williams, Allan Cluquot

FROM: Sam Ballard

DATE: February 5, 1996

TIME: 2:00 - 5:00 PM

PLACE: Conference Room B

Agenda Items	Time

1. *Review the agenda, agree on time frames and processes*
Post agenda with time frames
  a. Review agenda, time frames and processes. (5 minutes)
  b. Review all available statistical data. (20 minutes)
  c. Determine data most pertinent to management team. (60 minutes)
  d. Break (10 minutes)
  e. Calculate the numbers and begin to plan the presentation. (30 minutes)
  f. Check consistency of the big picture. (20 minutes)
  g. Determine who will give the presentation to management. (5 minutes)
  h. Determine when presenters will run through their presentation with this group. (5 minutes)
  i. Evaluate the meeting. (10 minutes)
	5 minutes
	2:00-2:05

2. *Review all available statistical data*
  a. Individuals list all statistics they collected on flip charts; include names of who gave them data and any assumptions made. (10 minutes)
  b. Briefly share information with others; individuals report back. (10 minutes)
	20 minutes
	2:05-2:25

3. *Determine what data are most pertinent to management team* a. Brainstorm what types of data will be most important to the management team. *"What will it take to convince them that our case is a sound one?"* (15 minutes) *(continued)*	60 minutes 2:25-3:25

Figure 2-2. Modified agenda for Sam's meeting.

b. Agree on what numbers/data are the most applicable for the presentation. *"We need to make a strong but honest case."* (20 minutes)	
c. Discuss any other concerns the management team will have. *"What else is happening in the business that we need to consider?" "What difficult questions will we likely encounter?"* (10 minutes)	
d. Determine how to address/incorporate those concerns. (15 minutes)	
4. *Break*	10 minutes 3:25-3:35
5. *Calculate the numbers and begin to plan the presentation.* a. Determine small groups to create the statistics. Select two individuals to work on the introduction and close of the presentation and to articulate the overall rationale for the change. [The statistics will build and support that rationale.] (5 minutes) b. Small groups work on calculating statistics and determining how to visually present them. One works on introduction, closing and business case. (15 minutes) c. Reports back: introduction, statistics/business case, closing. Each presented with draft of visual aids. (10 minutes)	30 minutes 3:35-4:05
6. *Check consistency of the big picture.* *"How well do these statistics work together to create a consistent and compelling story?"* (10 minutes) *"What is the best flow of our presentation?"* Place all visuals in sequence to create the story line. (10 minutes)	20 minutes 4:05-4:25
7. *Determine which people are most appropriate to give the presentation to management.* These people will go away to plan, practice, and present the actual presentation.	5 minutes 4:25-4:30
8. *Determine when to have presenters do a run-through of their presentation with this group.* (At least a half day before the actual presentation.)	5 minutes 4:30-4:35
9. *Evaluate the meeting.* What went well, opportunities for improvement.	10 minutes 4:35-4:45

Figure 2-2. *(Continued)*

- What specific issues or agenda items need to be addressed?
- What information needs to be gathered before the meeting?
- How should this information be gathered and by whom?
- How should this information be prepared and compiled for the meeting?
- Who should attend this meeting?
- Of these people, does everyone need to attend the entire meeting?
- How should the agenda be ordered to ensure that everyone's time is used wisely?
- What is the best date and location for the meeting?
  With ongoing groups, plan the time and place of your next meeting at the end of the previous meeting whenever possible.
- What correspondence should be sent to the participants before the meeting?

THE AGENDA ITEM QUESTIONS

- What is the overall purpose of each issue or agenda item?
  Because this information will be transferred directly to your agenda, structure each issue or agenda item as a statement that clearly expresses both its subject and purpose. For example: "Tax Report" only states the subject of the agenda item, and is therefore potentially confusing. "Decide How to Improve the Tax Report" is much clearer because it describes both the subject and purpose. Defining this purpose also provides a framework for answering the following agenda item questions. Include the people you selected to help in your meeting planning and rely on their feedback to help you make your decisions. If there are issues or agenda items not worthy of meeting time, now is the time to eliminate them.

- How, specifically, will each issue or agenda item be accomplished?
  Envision exactly how the meeting conversations will flow, what questions will need to be answered, and what problems might occur. Identify and isolate the resulting substeps of each issue or agenda item and break everything down into its smallest component.

- What are the most appropriate facilitation techniques for each substep?
  Refer to the corresponding "how to" chapters to identify specific techniques that will support you through the substeps of your agenda. If you are not sure how to proceed, ask yourself what is the purpose of each substep and which chapter best correlates with that purpose.

  Note that not every substep will require a specific technique. Sometimes, for example, simple group discussion will be adequate. Make sure that you are choosing techniques because they are the best techniques, not because they are the ones you feel most comfortable with.

- What meeting productivity techniques are required for this meeting?
  See Chap. 3 for ideas on controlling meeting behavior, keeping your meeting on track, improving the clarity of communication, stimulating and maintaining energy, and increasing participation.

- What are the time requirements for each issue or agenda item?

    Time requirements are based on the estimated time to complete each sub-step within an issue or agenda item. To accurately estimate meeting time, it is extremely important to break each agenda item down into its smallest possible substeps for analysis. Imagine how the discussions, exercises, and techniques you have selected will transpire. Design the agenda in such a way that you can control the momentum, yet be flexible enough to accommodate the inevitable timing errors built into your agenda. Include enough time in the agenda for any productivity techniques you plan to use from Chap. 3.

- What handouts, overheads, and other visual aids need to be prepared?

- Who should facilitate or present each issue or agenda item?

    The meeting facilitator or group manager is not always the appropriate person to be responsible for the meeting or for each specific agenda item. Delegate and share responsibility as much as possible.

- How should each issue or agenda item be introduced?

    Determine what background information participants will need. Consider using 3P STATEMENTS, Technique 8, as your introduction.

THE LOGISTICAL QUESTIONS

- What room arrangements and other preparations are necessary?

    _____ Audio-visual equipment?

    _____ Computer support?

    _____ Charts and easels? How many?

    _____ Tables, chairs? (Numbers and configurations)

    _____ Microphones? Fixed or roving?

    _____ Satellite/video/audio links?

    _____ Translations?

    _____ Car parking?

    _____ Flowers/music?

    _____ Travel arrangements?

    _____ Accessibility for the disabled?

    _____ Phone/fax availability?

    _____ Name tags/tents?

    _____ Arrangements for messages?

    _____ Other

- What refreshments should be served?

    _____ Catering?

    _____ Special food requirements?

- What level of documentation is necessary?
- What is the best way to arrange for minutes to be documented and distributed?

THE EVALUATION QUESTIONS
- What is the best way to evaluate the effectiveness of your meetings?
  See Chap. 9 for ideas.

STEP TWO: CREATING AN AGENDA

Many experts would argue that the meeting agenda, if properly prepared, is the most important and powerful component of any meeting. It is, at the very least, your road map to success. The agenda is a fundamental and essential element of every meeting, and serves as your preparation tool and script notes.

Once the Premeeting Planning Questions have been answered, you can effectively and almost effortlessly build your agenda. This process includes:

- Finalizing the order and flow of the agenda
- Reviewing the selected techniques, processes, and time frames for each agenda item
- Identifying alternative techniques in the event they are needed
- Physically preparing the final agenda document
- Obtaining final input or approval from key participants
- Distributing the agenda to all participants

Using the chart in Fig. 2-3 as a model, prepare your agenda. Remember that all of the information required to complete your agenda, except perhaps the final order of agenda items, has already been collected in your Premeeting Planning Questions. When considering the most suitable order for your agenda, rely on your logic and the input from others you have involved in the planning process. Keep in mind the primary goal of the meeting and diversify the tasks and pace to keep things fresh. It is a good idea to create a master template for a meeting agenda on your computer that you can customize every time you plan a meeting.

To be consistently successful, you should prepare two different agendas for each of your meetings. That's right, two! Prepare one for your meeting participants, which will be basically the same agenda you display during the meeting. Also prepare a more detailed agenda for yourself as a leader's guide. This is an easy and very useful process. The two agendas are more or less identical except for one thing. The participant version of the agenda usually excludes the specific details of the facilitation techniques you will utilize in your meeting. Your version is far more detailed in that it includes all the elements of the specific techniques you will employ for each agenda item.

The process of preparing two separate agendas is an example of another significant planning difference that separates the amateurs in business from the true

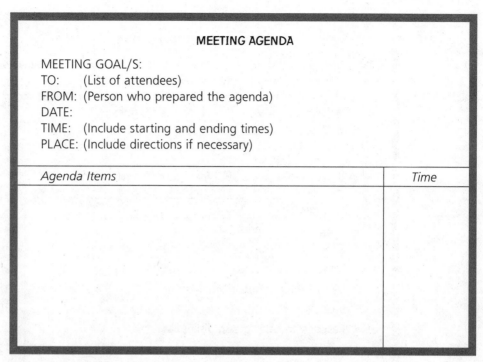

MEETING AGENDA

MEETING GOAL/S:
TO: (List of attendees)
FROM: (Person who prepared the agenda)
DATE:
TIME: (Include starting and ending times)
PLACE: (Include directions if necessary)

Agenda Items	Time

Figure 2-3. Meeting agenda template.

professionals. Figures 2-4 and 2-5 are examples for a meeting, Fig. 2-4 representing a completed meeting agenda that the participants see, and Fig. 2-5 depicting the corresponding meeting facilitator's agenda or leader's guide. When several people will be leading different portions of your meeting, consider expanding your agenda by adding a "who" column, as shown in these examples.

Now you're galloping on the fast track to meeting success. If you feel that this level of detail is overkill, question your paradigms. The irony is that the more detailed your facilitation planning becomes, the less bogged down in detail your meeting will actually be.

It may seem like a long and involved process but, if you follow the foregoing procedures, all of your hard work will result in a finished and professional meeting agenda. Remember to gain approval for your completed agenda from the key participants, and to distribute the document well in advance of the meeting.

PREPARING THE MEETING ENVIRONMENT

Communication experts state that nonverbal communication is 55 percent of the total message. If your physical environment is not conducive to productivity and creativity, the chances of your meeting accomplishing these goals are slim. Think about

MEETING AGENDA

MEETING GOAL/S: To create a shared understanding of the why, what, and how of the New Product development team.

TO: Brett Phillipson, Omar Ismat, Ian Pate, Martha D'Alessandro, Blair Dee, Sarah Vigil, Joseph Nguyen, James Hollows

FROM: Jessica Landry

DATE: March 14, 1996

TIME: 9:00-11:30 AM

PLACE: Away Inn, Hwy. 99, Emerald conference room

Agenda Items	Time
1. Welcoming remarks.	20 minutes
2. Review the history of how this idea came to be.	10 minutes
3. Understand the role of this team.	20 minutes
4. Discuss information in small groups.	15 minutes
5. Break.	10 minutes
6. Respond to small group discussions.	20 minutes
7. Describe the major components in the process.	15 minutes
8. Agree on the next steps.	20 minutes
9. Plan the next meeting.	5 minutes
10. Evaluate the meeting.	15 minutes

Figure 2-4. Participants' meeting agenda.

the difference in atmosphere between a sandwich shop and a gourmet restaurant. The moment you walk through the door you instantly get a feel for the type of meal you will have. The same is true when you walk into a meeting room.

Ensure that the physical environment for all your meetings is properly prepared. This doesn't mean that your preparation has to be expensive. It simply means that you should make a conscientious effort to provide a meeting environment that feels good to both you and your participants.

Windows

Some people believe that windows distract participants from discussions and the agenda at hand. In fact, the opposite is true. Natural light can have a wonderful effect on productivity. Whenever possible, open the shades. This creates an open feeling, ready for fresh air and fresh ideas.

MEETING AGENDA WITH FACILITATION NOTES

MEETING GOAL/S: To create a shared understanding of the why, what, and how of the New Product development team.

TO: Brett Phillipson, Omar Ismat, Ian Pate, Martha D'Alessandro, Blair Dee, Sarah Vigil, Joseph Nguyen, James Hollows

FROM: Jessica Landry

DATE: March 14, 1996

TIME: 9:00-11:30 AM

PLACE: Away Inn, Hwy. 99, Emerald conference room

Agenda Items	Time
1. *Welcoming remarks.* ■ Opening remarks from the divisional director (5 minutes) ■ Review the agenda [prepared chart] (2 minutes) ■ Introductions: [prepared chart] (10 minutes); name, job, fun fact ■ Review the ground rules [prepared chart; see Technique 3 for ideas] (3 minutes)	20 minutes 9:00-9:20
2. *Review the history of how this idea came to be.* Review history [use overhead] Outline the five major steps and time frames [another overhead]	10 minutes 9:20-9:30
3. *Understand the role of this team.* Answer these questions using visual aids/handouts ■ Why have a team? ■ Why were you in particular asked to participate? ■ What will you be responsible to do? ■ How much time will it take? ■ What are the expected results?	20 minutes 9:30-9:50
4. *Discuss information in small groups.* Ask participants to break into two small groups of four. Explain purpose [to have a few minutes to discuss what we covered so far among yourselves] and instructions (3 minutes). *Instructions:* ■ Pick a recorder (2 minutes)	15 minutes 9:50-10:05 (continued)

Figure 2-5. Facilitator's agenda for meeting.

■ Discuss: What are your reactions? and What are your questions? (10 minutes) ■ Recorder writes responses on sticky notes, one per sticky note. Puts sticky notes on premade charts near the door on the way out for break [Post instructions on chart paper]	
5. *Break.* Cluster sticky note responses into logical grouping during the break.	10 minutes 10:05-10:15
6. *Respond to the small group discussions.* Summarize reactions and answer questions from small group discussions.	20 minutes 10:15-10:35
7. *Describe the major components in the process.* Review the five major components and timeframes. Explain all components in some detail, especially the immediate next steps. [Use two overheads as visuals] Remember to ask for questions and concerns.	15 minutes 10:35-10:50
8. *Agree on the next steps.* Describe what must be done before the next meeting. [Use overhead as visual] (5 minutes) Brainstorm who should do what. [Chart responses] (5 minutes) Agree on individual or small working groups. [Chart responses] (5 minutes) Answer questions and concerns. (5 minutes)	20 minutes 10:50-11:10
9. *Plan the next meeting.* Determine where to meet and when.	5 minutes 11:10-11:15
10. *Evaluate the meeting.* Summarize what was covered in the meeting. Refer to the posted agenda. (1 minute) Chart the group's comments to these questions. (10 minutes) What went well? What are our opportunities for improvement for our next meeting? Summary remarks from the director. (4 minutes)	15 minutes 11:15-11:30

Figure 2-5. *(Continued)*

Atmosphere

Create as bright and energetic an atmosphere as possible. Add life and color to your meeting rooms by hanging pictures and posters, or even attaching kites to the ceiling or walls. Bring in plants or flowers. Consider playing music in the background before your meetings begin and during breaks. Use your imagination and common sense, and remember that a dull room can result in dull minds.

Room arrangement

Strive for a room arrangement that is conducive to discussion. The goal is for everyone to be able to have eye contact with everyone else. A meeting in auditorium style nonverbally communicates to your participants that they are there to hear a lecture. Refer to Fig. 2-6 for seating options.

Remember to arrange for chairs that will be comfortable for many hours of use and will provide proper physical support.

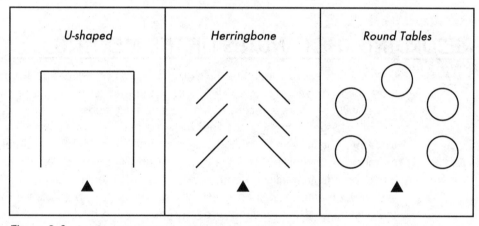

Figure 2-6. Seating options for participative meetings.

Temperature

Do your best to reserve a room where the participants can control the temperature thermostat themselves. Participants who are too hot or too cold will not be able to focus on the meeting agenda.

Food and beverages

It is often a good idea to include food and beverages in your meetings. Because sugar causes a quick energy high followed by a long crash, try to avoid it. If your group can't resist doughnuts and brioches, be sure to include lighter foods such as fruit or muffins. Those participants on special diets will appreciate the options. If you plan to provide coffee, be sure to provide tea, water, and possibly soft drinks as well. Place the food and beverages near the door, on the table, or where people will feel comfortable serving themselves during the meeting.

Interruptions

Plan for a method to assure that there are no interruptions, except for emergencies. This means a method to take messages at off-site locations, and a "no interruptions" policy inside the meetings. See GROUND RULES, Technique 3, for details on how to implement a "no interruptions" policy.

Setting the stage

Plan to arrive at the meeting location early to make sure that everything is set up the way you expected. Prepare your charts and other visual aids, and take care of any last minute details. Meet and greet people as they arrive. Take a few minutes to chat with participants and address any questions or concerns before the meeting begins. You will find that this added preparation time will help you feel more relaxed, set a positive and productive tone for the meeting, and increase your overall effectiveness.

RECORDING THE MINUTES OF THE MEETING

Determine ahead of time what level of detail will be needed in the meeting minutes. Some meeting groups will require a detailed record of all discussions while others will only want a record of actions and next steps.

For longer meetings, consider having an administrative assistant in the room to record the meeting highlights in real time. A portable computer is the best method for minimizing effort and maximizing time effectiveness. The electronic white boards that allow board notes to be printed on paper also work well. Whichever method you choose, establish who will be responsible for the minutes at the beginning of the meeting or before the meeting begins.

Distribute the minutes as quickly as possible after the meeting. Meeting results lose momentum when there are no notes to quickly reinforce decisions and actions. The minutes will make more sense and be far more valuable if delivered in or near real time. It should never take more than a few days to process and deliver them. If your meeting lasts more than one day, such as in a retreat, providing real-time minutes gives your participants an opportunity to refer to these notes as an effective method of review and preparation for the next session.

MORE INSIDE INFORMATION

Even though you have planned your meeting down to the minute, rest assured that things will never go exactly as planned. Agenda items and their issues will sometimes take more time and sometimes less, an important person to your meeting's success will not show up or have to leave early, or something critical will happen in the organization that overrides your original agenda. You will see signs of boredom, frustration, and interpersonal conflict that you have not planned for and will need to address.

Does this mean that planning is a waste of time? Quite the opposite! Your planning will give you an educated basis for making decisions about how best to move forward, and will help you negotiate changes with the participants as necessary. The more techniques you know and the more experience you have, the better able you will be to remain flexible and effective in the real world of your meetings.

Be open to change, and don't be afraid to make the uncomfortable statement or ask the difficult question. You will almost always find that your flexibility and courage are appreciated and respected. For example, you might observe,

> *It seems that Joan and Enrique have some strong disagreements about this topic. Is it best for us all to continue this debate or would it be more appropriate for the two of the them to continue their discussion after the meeting?*
>
> *Some of you are looking confused. What can we do to make things clearer?*
>
> *This conversation is taking longer than I anticipated. Should we continue and postpone another part of the agenda to another date, wrap this conversation up, or continue our meeting past its deadline?*

Just remember to make all changes openly and always allow your meeting group to participate in making the decisions.

Continual improvement

Take a few minutes after each meeting to review what went well and what you would do differently if you had it to do again. Jot down a few specific notes. This quick and simple process, combined with the formal feedback you receive from your meeting participants, will help you to continually improve your effectiveness as a meeting facilitator.

Changing your style

If you have a history of dull, autocratic meetings and now suddenly decide to change your style, discuss the changes you propose with your meeting groups first. Ask for their input and ideas. If you change without proactively saying something, people are likely to be resistant and highly suspicious.

Consider meeting alternatives

Even the best-run meeting can be a waste of time if it is not necessary in the first place. Following are some questions to ask yourself before even calling a meeting:

- Is a meeting the most effective way to accomplish the goals of each proposed agenda item?
- Is everyone necessary to the success of the meeting going to be there?
- Do all those invited to the meeting have to be there?
- What meeting alternatives have I considered?

You might decide, based on the given situation, to invite some people for only part of the meeting, meet with participants one on one, gather the necessary information through E-mail, or just send a memo and ask for written input. Always keep in mind that your ultimate goal is to work for the success and best interests of the organization you serve. And that means that meetings are not always the best answer.

IN SUMMARY

It is your responsibility as a meeting facilitator to make your meetings as successful as possible. This process begins with the Premeeting Planning Questions discussed in this chapter and leads to the creation of a two-level meeting agenda that will smoothly and systematically move your group from issue to issue. As a part of this process, you select and apply the most appropriate meeting facilitation techniques described in this book and prepare a meeting environment that is conducive to productivity, creativity, and participation. Sometimes these efforts are relatively simple and other times they are difficult and stressful. But it can be done!

It is important to remember that the quality of any meeting and its agenda are relative to the quality of information you collect during the Premeeting Planning Questions stage. If you don't include others in your planning, the value of the information you gather will be negatively impacted. If you don't clearly define the purpose and goals of your meeting, time will be wasted. If you don't labor over the issues and details of each proposed agenda item, the techniques you select might not work effectively and your timelines may be unpredictable.

The step-by-step approach detailed in this chapter breaks the meeting down into its constituent parts and provides a template for success. Unfortunately, it can't insure the perfect meeting. It can't specifically illustrate the interplay and improvisation that ultimately weaves and melds these constituent parts together. There is not an absolute formula for this process. Every meeting is different, every meeting group is different, every meeting facilitator is different, and the general content and dynamics of every situation are different. But with the proper motivation, flexibility, and expertise, the skills and techniques provided in this text will give you a strong foundation to work from. It is your commitment, ability, expertise, and personality that will define how you will draw all the pieces of each meeting puzzle together. Sometimes you may even create a meeting masterpiece.

3

20 Techniques to Improve Meeting Productivity

Everyone on Anne's manufacturing team is complaining about having to attend another one of her meetings. *"Why should we go? Nothing ever gets accomplished. Most of us just sit there and waste away while she tries to control totally meaningless and unfocused conversations, bickering, and finger pointing. It's a waste of time!"*

Anne couldn't agree more. *"It's obvious that everybody, including me, is frustrated. I just don't know where to start!"*

Joe's group is light-years ahead of Anne's. *"We have a great organization! Everybody works well together and is committed to continual improvement. And we've seen the value of participation in our improved performance! This year we're targeting our meetings as an area for improvement and are eager to learn new techniques to help us reach our goals. But we're not sure how to begin."*

This chapter outlines the twenty fundamental facilitation techniques that are basic to meeting success. These essential productivity techniques provide specific, uncomplicated processes to define meeting behavior, keep meetings on track, improve the clarity of communication, and maintain maximum energy. Employing these procedures not only saves time and increases effectiveness and efficiency, but also adds immediate power to every meeting agenda by eliminating time wasters, focusing discussions, expanding the quality of input, and significantly increasing participation.

The specific techniques for defining and controlling meeting behavior include:

- 1 INTRODUCTIONS
- 2 CLEARING
- 3 GROUND RULES
- 4 PULSE CHECK

For keeping your meeting on track, use:

- 5 UNFINISHED BUSINESS
- 6 VERBAL WARNINGS

- 7 THE BELL
- 8 3P STATEMENTS
- 9 SHREDDED QUESTIONS
- 10 SELF-MANAGEMENT
- 11 GO/NO GO

For improving the clarity of communication, apply:

- 12 CHARTING
- 13 ART
- 14 ANALOGIES AND METAPHORS

When you want to stimulate and keep the energy high, utilize:

- 15 BREAKS
- 16 MOVEMENT
- 17 TOYS
- 18 MUSIC

When you want to increase participation, employ:

- 19 WRITING
- 20 SMALL GROUPS

1

INTRODUCTIONS

I want to be sure that everyone in our group is acquainted and feels comfortable with each other. How can I structure personal introductions to include the entire group, as well as add value to the participative process?

What is INTRODUCTIONS?

INTRODUCTIONS is a technique to assure that all participants know each other. Even in an organization where roles and responsibilities overlap and flex, people in your meeting want to know who is there and what they have to contribute. People will not work openly if they do not know who else is in the room.

INTRODUCTIONS is an activity that includes everyone at the beginning of your meeting. It creates an equal ground, and highlights the expectation of participation.

When do I use INTRODUCTIONS?

- When your meeting participants aren't acquainted with each other.
- When you want to increase participants' knowledge of each other.

How do I use INTRODUCTIONS?

1. <u>Include INTRODUCTIONS on your agenda.</u> Allow about one minute of time for each participant.

2. <u>Decide which type of introduction is most appropriate for your group.</u>

   Option A: *Tell us your name and something personal about yourself that most of the group doesn't know. For example, a hobby, something about your family, somewhere you have lived, etc.*

   Option B: *Tell us your name and what you do in two sentences.*

   Option C: *Pair up with someone you don't know and haven't met yet. Introduce yourselves and talk for a few minutes to get to know each other better. Then you will introduce each other to the group.*

   Suggest some guidelines, such as questions to ask from options A and B.

   Note: Allow an extra five to seven minutes for this option.

   Option D: *Please share your name, background, and what skills you have that will contribute to the meeting, e.g., expertise in operations, budgeting.*

Note: This option is especially pertinent as groups form on quality improvement or for new boards of directors.

Note: Options A through D can be combined with MOVEMENT, Technique 16, where a ball is thrown from person to person during their INTRODUCTIONS.

Option E: When there is a new person added to a group that already know each other, you can say:

I would like to introduce (the person's name). (The person's name) *comes to us from* (the place, company, or division), *where she was responsible for* (whatever the person was responsible for). *I'm sure* (the person's name) *will be a positive addition to our group, with her expertise in* (specific skills, expertise).

You can then ask the person to add to what has been said. Ask all other participants to introduce themselves.

3. Use INTRODUCTIONS as planned.

2

CLEARING

It seems that when our meetings begin, everybody's minds are still focused on what they just left behind: their work, their weekend, their vacation, or whatever. It really takes a long time for us all to get settled. What can we do to get focused sooner?

What is CLEARING?

CLEARING is a productivity technique that allows the members of your group to clear their minds and focus on the meeting. It provides a transition from what they just left behind to the meeting itself. CLEARING significantly decreases the time it takes participants to settle themselves at the beginning of the meeting, providing earlier focus and greater effectiveness.

This technique involves participants' sharing what they are thinking about with the meeting group. Once a person has voiced what is on his or her mind, these thoughts are more easily put aside. You may have noticed this in your own life. For example, after sharing your frustration about a current project with a colleague, you find that your frustration diminishes and you are better able to focus on your work. Left unacknowledged, your frustration mounts, further impeding your effectiveness. One-on-one meetings usually allow a few minutes of this "How's it going?" informal conversation before focusing on the formal topic. Group meetings usually do not have this CLEARING time built in. As a result, meeting participants take longer to settle into the formal business at hand.

CLEARING also allows participants to let the other meeting members know in a constructive way if anything is getting in the way of 100 percent participation.

The goal of CLEARING is not to solve problems or address the concerns that arise, but rather to allow people to simply state their issues. The few moments of venting time provided by this technique effectively helps people focus and concentrate on the meeting sooner.

CLEARING will not be enough to totally transform the effectiveness of your meetings. You will want to use a variety of other techniques as well. These techniques will vary depending on the group and the specific agenda of the meeting. However, the CLEARING technique, coupled with GROUND RULES, Technique 3, usually provides a solid foundation for focused meetings.

When do I use CLEARING?

- When participants' other obligations keep their minds on topics other than the meeting.

- When participants come to the meeting without taking a few minutes to relax or talk together informally.

How do I use CLEARING?

1. Explain to participants the purpose of CLEARING. For example:

CLEARING is a technique for transitioning from your previous thoughts and activities to our meeting. If you agree, we'll use CLEARING at the beginning of each meeting to help us get focused more quickly. The goal of CLEARING is not to solve problems, but instead to simply state what you have on your mind. By doing so, you are better able to put those issues aside and give your full attention to the meeting.

2. Explain the instructions for CLEARING. Post the instructions on a chart or overhead, as in Fig. 3-1.

CLEARING INSTRUCTIONS

- Everyone gets a turn.
- One minute maximum per person.
- Briefly share issues, positive or negative, currently on your mind.
- Use statements instead of questions.
- Listen without problem solving.
- It's OK to pass or say, "I'm clear."
- Keep it quick.

Figure 3-1. Instructions chart for CLEARING.

3. Begin the CLEARING exercise. Be sure everyone gets a turn. The first time you may want to start, thus giving the other participants an example to follow.

Option: If your group is large, ask participants to clear informally with others next to them. If people are sitting at tables, each table can "clear" independently.

Note: If someone brings up an issue worthy of group discussion, put it on your UNFINISHED BUSINESS chart, Technique 5, or otherwise note it for later discussion. Unless there is some emergency, like an impending lawsuit or supplier disaster, do not change your agenda to accommodate these issues. It would be rare for serious problems to come up in the CLEARING session. Simple venting and sharing of personal news will be more common. For example:

Our department's financial report is due in two weeks, and we have two months of data to analyze. Needless to say, I'm feeling a little stress.

We just won the Edmondson account. We've been working on them for over a year, and their business will put us in line for winning their parent company's business next year.

I'm having problems with my back again. Please excuse me if I stand up during parts of the meeting. Sitting exacerbates the problem.

4. <u>After everyone has had a turn, thank the group and move on to the next agenda item.</u>

Note: The first time you use CLEARING with a specific group, note that you will ask for feedback about the technique at the end of the meeting. By then the group will be able to see if CLEARING helped the session run more smoothly. At the end of the meeting, take a few minutes to ask the group:

What were your observations about our meeting effectiveness?

What value did CLEARING add?

Do you think we should keep CLEARING as a regular exercise?

Note: With agreement from your group, start each meeting with a brief CLEARING session.

Option: Use CLEARING sporadically, when participants seem to be restless at the beginning of the meeting.

3

GROUND RULES

Sometimes people act inappropriately at our meetings. They come in late, interrupt others, ramble from topic to topic, dominate discussions, are hostile to the ideas and opinions of others, and have side conversations. Is there an easy way to handle these situations?

What is GROUND RULES?

GROUND RULES is a productivity technique for establishing and maintaining acceptable standards of meeting behavior. Using this technique virtually eliminates behavioral problems before they begin. When behavioral problems do occur, preestablished GROUND RULES support your request for change.

This technique involves discussing and posting the resulting meeting GROUND RULES in such a way as to constantly remind meeting participants of the rules and regulations of their meeting.

If standards of behavior are not discussed and agreed upon ahead of time, it is very difficult to censure a person's behavior. This is because acceptable and unacceptable behaviors have never been defined. GROUND RULES provides this definition and becomes the group's standard of behavior. The technique enhances productivity and participation, and helps keep the meeting on track.

When do I use GROUND RULES?

- When you want to use your meeting time wisely.
- When you expect conflict because of specific personalities or volatile issues.
- When the group has a lot to accomplish in a short period of time.
- When there is a history of unproductive behavior at previous meetings.
- When a group is working together for the first time.

How do I use GROUND RULES?

1. **At your meeting,** introduce the idea and state the purpose of having GROUND RULES. For example:

   GROUND RULES is designed to act as an agreement outlining how we will conduct ourselves during the meeting. Once we agree, we will post our GROUND RULES near the front of the room and refer to them as needed. Anyone can remind us of our GROUND RULES if they see that we are getting off track.

Note: If you want to establish GROUND RULES with a pre-existing group, talk with the group, or at least a sampling of participants, about the idea before you put the issue on the agenda. For example:

It seems to me that we have established some unproductive norms, such as jumping from subject to subject, starting late, etc. (Use your own meetings' examples without pointing fingers.) I would like to take a few minutes at our next meeting to determine what standards we would like to establish for ourselves in the future. What do you think of this idea?

2. Using chart paper, <u>show the group sample GROUND RULES,</u> as in Fig. 3-2.
3. <u>Ask the group what GROUND RULES they would like to use as their own.</u> Chart (write down on chart paper) their ideas.

   Option A: Use a fresh piece of paper to chart their ideas.

   Option B: Leave plenty of room on the page of example GROUND RULES you presented. Write modifications and additions directly on that page.
4. When you and your group feel that the list of GROUND RULES is complete, <u>ask if there are any GROUND RULES that anyone cannot live with or support.</u> Change them as necessary. Be sure that everyone agrees to all GROUND RULES.

EXAMPLES OF GROUND RULES

(Your own list should not be this long.)

- Listen to and honor all opinions and concerns
- One conversation at a time
- Focus on the task at hand
- Avoid outside distractions
- Work toward honest consensus
- Fun is allowed
- Think "out of the box"
- Help us stay on track and on schedule
- Avoid detail overload, keep remarks brief and to the point
- Avoid personal agendas
- Stay future-oriented, don't dwell on the past
- Offer solutions, not complaints
- All items written on charts as a record
- No lectures
- Cellular phones off; pagers on pulse

Figure 3-2. GROUND RULES samples.

Note: In potentially volatile situations, ask each person individually, in "round robin" fashion, if he or she is willing to personally support the GROUND RULES.

5. <u>Ask participants what measures they, as a group, think should be taken if the GROUND RULES are not followed.</u>
   This helps secure agreement on how to handle potential problems if they occur, and makes everyone responsible for meeting success. Agree on something that fits the personality of the group, can be done by any participant, and serves as clear and immediate feedback. For example, one group agreed to point in the direction of the posted GROUND RULES as a nonverbal reminder. Another group decided to use a more direct approach and created this formula:

   We agreed to (indicate the pertinent GROUND RULE). *It seems that we're/you're* (state the disruptive behavior). *What do you think?*

   Here are two specific examples:

   We agreed to avoid detail overload. It seems as if you are giving us more information than we need at this point. What do you think?

   We agreed to listen to and honor all opinions and concerns. It seems that you are not taking Julie's perspective seriously. What is your perspective?

6. <u>Post the GROUND RULES</u> in a prominent place at every meeting held with that same group. (The chart may need to be rewritten if your original is too messy.)

7. <u>Refer to the GROUND RULES as needed</u> and review them when new members join the group. Modify them as necessary.

4

PULSE CHECK

I know that from time to time there is some skepticism within our group. But I don't know how to identify which specific issues are causing the most concern and how much our success is impacted. I wish I had a way of measuring the attitudes of our group. Do you have any ideas?

What is PULSE CHECK?

PULSE CHECK is a technique to determine the mood, attitude, temperature, or "pulse" of your group.

PULSE CHECK involves asking individuals to articulate their feelings toward a particular issue. Their ratings are used to determine the overall "pulse" of the group and act as a springboard for discussion about how people are feeling and why.

Negativity, left unchecked, can feed on itself. And what may start with one or two people can quickly spread to the rest of the group. For this reason, it is wise to identify and address any concerns proactively. PULSE CHECK information will help identify any possible negative energy surrounding an issue and support its transformation into a positive force from the start. Because PULSE CHECK will also expose positive attitudes, it can help you sustain positive energy.

This technique should be used to help you "feel the pulse" of your group on an issue, positive or negative, so that you can use it to the group's greatest advantage and benefit.

When do I use PULSE CHECK?

- When you want to know the "pulse" of your group about a specific issue.
- When you suspect that there will be low energy and enthusiasm for your meeting.
- When the group has had negative experiences in the past and you want to stimulate more positive experiences in the future.

How do I use PULSE CHECK?

1. Introduce the PULSE CHECK. For example:

   Let's take our group 'pulse' by identifying our present attitudes about xxxx (xxxx being the specific issue, concern, or even the meeting itself). We will do this by secret ballot and tally. Then we will have a brief discussion of our findings. There we will look for ways to turn any negative energy or concerns toward a positive outcome.

2. Gather "pulse ratings" from each individual at the meeting.

    a. Pass out small pieces of paper to all participants and ask participants to select a number from 1 (low) to 10 (high) that reflects their expectations for a successful outcome about the issue at hand. Have them write this number on the paper.

        Note: You may participate unless you are a neutral facilitator.

        Option: If the group has a high level of trust, ask for verbal reports or ask each person to come forward to 'record' his or her number on the chart.

    b. Ask participants to fold their papers and pass them to one or two designated people near the front of the room.

        Note: Designate people who are in a logical location for this. You could also ask participants to pass their paper to persons in corner points of the room, or to a designated person at each table. Do what seems logical given the layout of your room and the size of your group.

    c. Ask the designated people to read the numbers aloud. Record numbers by adding tick marks on a prepared chart similar to Fig. 3-3.

    d. Identify the group's average score. Add all the numbers together and divide by the total number of voters to arrive at the average score.

        Note: Unless you are quick at math, bring a calculator. If you don't have your calculator, ask another participant to do the math for you.

    e. Ask volunteers to give some specific reasons why they awarded the ratings that they did.

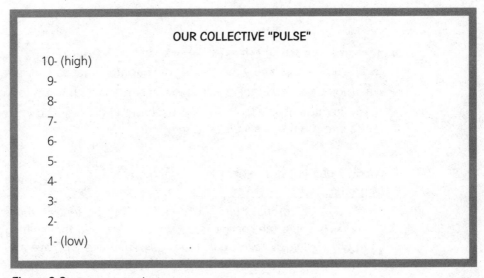

Figure 3-3. PULSE CHECK chart.

3. Discuss your group results.

    a. Ask the group, for example:

       What in particular stands out to you? What are your reactions to this information? How might these results impact our work together? What can we do to exceed the expectations of the group? How can we use this information to help us make our project more successful?

       Note: Modify these questions to best meet the specific needs of your group.

    b. Summarize the key points from the group discussion. Chart key points as appropriate.

4. Take action according to the suggestions of the group.

5

UNFINISHED BUSINESS

Our meetings are continually spinning off onto tangents unrelated to our original agenda. We never accomplish what we originally set out to do and everyone is frustrated, including me. What can I do?

What is UNFINISHED BUSINESS?

UNFINISHED BUSINESS is a productivity technique for effectively dealing with bothersome but important nonagenda items that arise during the course of your meeting.

Nonagenda items always seem to find their way into meetings. It is important to honor and recognize the existence of these nonagenda items, but without interrupting the focus and goals of your meeting agenda. UNFINISHED BUSINESS involves recording these tangential issues on paper, insuring that they will be remembered and addressed, but without interrupting the ongoing conversation.

UNFINISHED BUSINESS is another basic productivity technique that can be used to support your group's GROUND RULES, Technique 3, for keeping on track.

When do I use UNFINISHED BUSINESS?

- When the meeting gets off track with issues worthy of discussion or action but unrelated, or tangential, to the current agenda item.

How do I use UNFINISHED BUSINESS?

1. At or before the beginning of each meeting, <u>place a chart labeled UNFINISHED BUSINESS on the wall.</u> Refer to Fig. 3-4. The first time you use UNFINISHED BUSINESS explain its purpose to the participants at the beginning of your meeting. Gain their approval to use this technique as needed throughout the meeting. For example:

   As you know, our meetings often get off the subject and we end up spending our time on issues outside our agenda. I suggest that from now on, when this starts to happen, we chart the tangential issue on an UNFINISHED BUSINESS chart for later discussion. That way, we will remember to come back to the issue later, but still be able to accomplish our meeting's goals. What do you think? ... I encourage you all to help me note when our conversations are getting off track.

   Note: UNFINISHED BUSINESS comes under many other names. The Parking Lot, the Bin List, and the Flag List are examples. Find a name that your group likes and use it consistently.

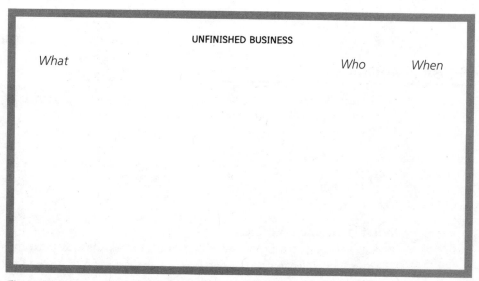

UNFINISHED BUSINESS

What   *Who*   *When*

Figure 3-4. UNFINISHED BUSINESS chart.

2. <u>When the conversation sways off track</u> with an issue worthy of consideration but off the topic under discussion, <u>briefly stop the meeting. Write a quick synopsis of the issue,</u> with permission from the group, <u>on the UNFINISHED BUSINESS chart.</u>

Note: If the issue is trivial, politely remind the group that the meeting is getting off track. If you are not sure if an issue is worthy of the UNFINISHED BUSINESS list, ask the group what they think.

3. As one of the last agenda items to your meeting, <u>go back to your UNFINISHED BUSINESS list. Decide, as a group, how to address each item.</u> Some issues may be appropriate for discussion at your next meeting. Others may be more appropriately handled by a subset of the group or even by an individual. Some issues will no longer seem important and will be dropped.

Note: During this discussion, document who will do what and by when. This ensures that issues will be addressed. For example:

Sam and Rebecca will make recommendations for new building site at next meeting. Carl to send information on product exposure through E-mail by Friday, 9/8.

Write the information directly on your UNFINISHED BUSINESS chart and include it in the minutes of your meeting.

Note: Be sure to save enough time at the end of your meeting for this step. If you fail to go back to UNFINISHED BUSINESS before the end of the meeting, you lose credibility. People will be reluctant to have their issues permanently left and forgotten on the UNFINISHED BUSINESS chart.

6

VERBAL WARNINGS

I agree that each agenda item should have a time limit but, as we get into our conversation, sometimes we forget how much time has gone by. More often than not, our allotted time is gone before we've come to any conclusions. How can we avoid this problem?

What is VERBAL WARNINGS?

VERBAL WARNINGS is a productivity technique to help groups pace their discussions. This technique involves verbalizing how much discussion or work time remains within a predetermined and agreed upon deadline.

Having time frames assigned to each agenda item is a great step toward enhancing meeting effectiveness. The VERBAL WARNINGS technique further increases meeting success by managing discussion time. It focuses discussions because it regulates the discussion clock, although this control feature must remain flexible enough to expand and contract as the specific discussion dictates.

By regulating the clock, this technique also gives the meeting facilitator a powerful tool to help accurately estimate time parameters for future meeting agendas.

When do I use VERBAL WARNINGS?

- When you want to keep your meetings on track.
- When you are nearing the completion of each item on your agenda.

How do I use VERBAL WARNINGS?

1. <u>Introduce the VERBAL WARNINGS technique and determine who will track the time at the beginning of each meeting.</u> The first time you use this technique, you might say, for example:

   In order to help us meet our agreed upon schedule, we need to keep better track of our time. I suggest that from now on, we ask one person to be our official timekeeper at every meeting. That person will be responsible to give us VERBAL WARNINGS about how much time we have left. For instance, in a discussion scheduled for 45 minutes, the timekeeper would give us 30-minute, 15-minute, 7-minute, and 2-minute warnings. If the timekeeper felt we were using our time wisely, they might only give us a 7-minute and a 2-minute warning instead. What do you think about the idea? ... Who would like to be our timekeeper today?

Note: Even if you are an external facilitator, it is generally better to share responsibility for the meeting's success by using a timekeeper.

Note: When small group discussions are used, each group elects its own timekeeper.

2. Give VERBAL WARNINGS for each agenda item as needed.

3. Negotiate times as necessary.

When the predetermined time is insufficient, ask the group or small groups how much more time they need. Negotiate with the participants for more time as is appropriate.

Note: This might mean negotiating not just how much time is needed for that agenda item, but also what other items will be dropped from that meeting's agenda.

Conversely, be sure to watch for opportunities when less time is needed for an agenda item than was originally planned. If you are observant and proactive in this way, your group will be able to use this extra time for other agenda items or meeting business.

7

THE BELL

I have trouble calling our meetings to order. My voice isn't easily heard when other people are talking, even with a microphone. This is a problem before we begin, when we come back from breaks, and when we are using small group discussions. I end up with a near case of laryngitis. There has to be an easier way.

What is THE BELL?
THE BELL is an effective and simple productivity technique to communicate to meeting participants that it is time to reconvene. Using THE BELL is one way of saving your voice and being heard above the crowd.

When do I use THE BELL?
- When you want to indicate that the meeting is starting.
- When you want to bring small groups back together into a large group again.
- When the situation has gotten out of control or off the subject.

How do I use THE BELL?
1. It is a good idea to <u>mention the purpose and use of THE BELL the first time you use it</u> with a meeting group. Be sure you <u>ask for the support of your participants</u> in helping you keep the meeting on schedule.

   Note: Purchase a small dinner bell or customer service bell for your meetings. Both are inexpensive and easy to locate. Customer services bells can typically be found at your local office supply store, but you can use any bell that is not too shrill and obnoxious. Be sure that your bell can be heard above the sound of participants' voices.

2. Simply <u>ring the bell</u> at all appropriate times <u>to reconvene your meeting group.</u>

8

3P STATEMENTS

PURPOSE
PROCESS
PAYOFF

Even though I think I've been clear, my meeting participants often question me about the specific function and value of things we are doing as a group. They certainly have every right to know what is going on and why. Is there a technique I can use to better explain what will happen, how it will happen, and why it will happen?

What is 3P STATEMENTS?

3P STATEMENTS is a productivity technique for explaining the focus, methodology, and value of a given upcoming agenda item. It informs your meeting group of what to expect and what will be accomplished from the start.

3P STATEMENTS is used to help a meeting group adequately prepare for the meeting itself, a presentation, a new agenda item, or a discussion topic. 3P is an acronym of sorts which translates into *purpose, process,* and *payoff*. The technique involves answering three basic and critical questions in statement form: What will we do? How will we do it? Why is it important?

Purpose states what you plan to accomplish. Stating this intention or purpose of a topic answers some fundamental questions. Why are we here? What is the goal? How will the information be used?

Process describes how the topic under consideration will be addressed, and answers additional important questions. How will we proceed? What techniques will we use? What steps will we take? How long will this last? What is expected of me? What is expected of the group?

Payoff informs your participants of the benefit, or what they will get from the discussion, and resolves the following questions: Why bother? What is in it for me to participate? What are the real benefits? How will this affect our group's goals?

Not only does the 3P STATEMENTS technique provide essential information to your meeting group, it also provides you as the facilitator with critical planning information. If you can't identify the *purpose, process,* and *payoff* for any given topic of discussion, do not proceed. If you do, the likelihood of failure will be high.

When do I use 3P STATEMENTS?

- When you are planning the agenda for your meeting.
- When you are starting your meeting.
- When you are beginning a new agenda item in your meeting.
- When you are making a formal presentation.

How do I use 3P STATEMENTS?

1. When planning your meeting, <u>apply the 3P STATEMENTS template to the proposed topics of your agenda:</u>

   a. What is the *purpose* of this topic?

   b. What *process* will we use to discuss it?

   c. What is the anticipated *payoff* (benefit or result) from the discussion?

   Consider using this template to organize your 3P STATEMENTS:

   In order to _____*(purpose)*_____, we will _____*(process)*_____, so that _____*(payoff)*_____.

   Note: Modify this template to meet your specific situation.

   An example using this format is:

   To decide how best to meet our customers' needs, we will conduct a focus group with our key customers. This will give us information on what they see as the top priorities for improvement in the next fiscal year.

2. <u>Use the 3P STATEMENTS as planned.</u>

   Note: Remember that 3P STATEMENTS can be used to help you plan your meeting agendas, open your meetings, introduce new agenda items during your meetings, or make formal presentations or suggestions.

9

SHREDDED QUESTIONS

It seems as if our meetings' conversations always go around in circles. We talk about different aspects of the same question all at the same time. Is there a specific technique we can use that will give us some structure and control over this?

AGENDA ITEM
1. Facts
2. Feelings
3. Brainstorming or creative alternatives
4. Pros of each alternative
5. Cons of each alternative
6. Agreement on a decision
7. Next steps

What is SHREDDED QUESTIONS?

SHREDDED QUESTIONS is a technique that outlines an orderly process for addressing a specific meeting issue or agenda item. This technique ensures that every facet of the specific issue under discussion will be examined thoroughly and efficiently.

Generally, the facets of meeting issues include:

- Facts
- Feelings
- Brainstorming or creative alternatives
- The pros of each alternative
- The cons of each alternative
- Agreement on the decision
- Next steps

Unstructured discussions can result in all seven of these facets being discussed simultaneously, and the consequences of this lack of structure are wasted time and disappointing results. SHREDDED QUESTIONS breaks each issue or agenda item down into a series of specific questions drawn from each of the seven facets. With this technique, discussions become ordered, focused, and more successful.

SHREDDED QUESTIONS saves valuable meeting time and dramatically improves the quality and the results of all meeting discussions where the technique is applied. This shredding technique also allows you as a facilitator to estimate agenda time lines more effectively.

When do I use SHREDDED QUESTIONS?

- When you want to examine all aspects of a specific issue or agenda item efficiently.
- When your group will be discussing complex issues.
- When discussions seem to go around in circles.

How do I use SHREDDED QUESTIONS?

BEFORE THE MEETING:

1. Determine the purpose and desired end result of your specific agenda item.
2. Determine the best questions to guide your proposed discussion.

a. Be sure to include questions that will consider all seven facets: facts, feelings, creative alternatives, the pros of each alternative, the cons of each alternative, agreement on the decisions, and next steps.

Note: Eliminate inappropriate categories based on the goal of that particular agenda item.

Facts include purely factual information. Save the analysis of the facts for later. Some example questions to elicit facts include:

What are the key points? What specific details do you recall? What are the numbers? What do the experts say? What are the facts?

Note: The facts are typically collected first and need to be comprehensive. Be sure to obtain them from all available perspectives, some of which may not be in your meeting. This step creates a foundation for all further discussion on the issue under consideration.

Feelings include intuitions, feelings, and emotional reactions. Sample questions might include:

What was the high point or low point for you? What was the collective mood at the time? How do you feel about it? What are you excited about? What are you worried about? What is your gut feeling?

Note: Emotions and feelings are important information. When taken into consideration, they strengthen and support decisions. If ignored they can jeopardize those decisions. It is imperative to include emotional information and energy along with the facts.

Creative Alternatives are the result of brainstorming, and offer the possible solutions to a given problem. Question examples include:

What alternatives do we have? What ideas do you have?

Note: Refer to THE OLD-FASHIONED WAY, Technique 28, or other specific brainstorming techniques described in Chap. 5.

The Pros of each alternative reveal the positive side of the brainstormed ideas. Ask, for example:

How will this make a difference in the way we do business? What are the positive aspects of this option? What are the benefits of this alternative?

The Cons of each alternative reveal the negative side of the brainstormed ideas. Questions you might ask include:

What are the negatives we should consider? What are the budgetary requirements? What are the personnel requirements?

Note: The last two questions could be perceived as either Pro or Con, depending on the situation.

Note: Both facts and feelings can be used to assess the viability of any creative alternative.

Agreement on the Decision, or decisions, should be reached by consensus, agreed upon, and mutually owned by all participants. To lead a group to a decision you might ask:

Now that we have analyzed all the information, what should we do? What is our decision?

Note: See Chap. 7, "11 Techniques to Make Decisions," for specific techniques to help your group make decisions.

Next Steps provides the follow-through to ensure that the decision (or decisions) taken is (are) effectively implemented and monitored. You might say, for example:

What are the next steps? Who do we need to communicate with? How will we measure our success? What are the steps we need to take to implement these changes? What can we do to make sure that the program is implemented properly?

Note: Consider MINDMAPPING, Technique 29, or CHART ACTIONS, Technique 64, as possibilities to support the Next Steps.

b. Develop no more than five to ten questions.

Note: There will probably be more questions required to determine facts than will be necessary for the other facets.

c. Be sure to use open-ended questions. See OPEN-ENDED QUESTIONS, Technique 34, for details.

3. Prepare any visual aids you will use in the meeting.

IN THE MEETING

1. Introduce the issue or agenda item for discussion. Describe the intended result and purpose. Explain why this issue is important.

2. Explain the SHREDDED QUESTIONS technique, and ask the group for their help in answering only one question at a time. You might say, for example:

Let's try to keep our discussion focused on one aspect of this issue at a time. Here are the questions I've prepared to help us accomplish this. (Display your questions on an overhead or chart.) I'd appreciate your help in answering the questions one by one. This will save us both time and frustration.

Note: Letting the group see all the questions from the beginning will help them focus and remain patient.

3. Lead the discussion, either as a large group or in small groups. Record the points of the discussion on charts. Post each chart so that it can be viewed throughout the meeting.

Note: Alter your preplanned questions if they are not working as expected. Ask your group for help in modifying the questions if necessary.

10

SELF-MANAGEMENT

How can I stimulate the participants in our group to become more involved and take more responsibility for our meeting's success?

What is SELF-MANAGEMENT?

SELF-MANAGEMENT is a productivity technique for stimulating participant involvement and sharing of responsibility and ownership for meeting success.

This is accomplished by breaking apart the different roles of the meeting facilitator and sharing them among the participants in the meeting. These roles include Leader, Recorder, Minute Taker, and Timekeeper, as well as Reporter in small group discussions.

When the facilitation duties are shared by group members, their involvement and ownership increases automatically. SELF-MANAGEMENT increases meeting success by sharing responsibility, and also stimulates better focus, commitment, and participation.

When do I use SELF-MANAGEMENT?

- When you want fuller group participation in your meetings.
- When you use small group discussions within your meetings.

How do I use SELF-MANAGEMENT?

1. Describe the SELF-MANAGEMENT technique and its purpose to the group. For example:

   We want our meetings to be more successful. As each person's involvement in the process increases, contribution and ownership increase as well. By breaking down and sharing the meeting facilitation roles, we can accomplish this result. What do you think? A successful meeting facilitator has several roles and responsibilities. These include: (Use a chart or overhead similar to Fig. 3-5.)

2. Select participants to fill the meeting roles. You might say, for example:

   In order to share responsibility for the success of our meeting, I'd like to suggest that at each meeting we rotate these roles. What do you think? I've planned to lead this meeting, but who would like to be our Recorder? our Minute Taker? our Timekeeper? Thanks everyone. Let's see how our meeting runs with this new shared responsibility.

```
                        MEETING ROLES

    Leader: Facilitates the meeting. Takes a leadership role in planning the
    meeting.
    Recorder: Records all comments, ideas, and decisions on chart paper.
    Minute Taker: Prepares the minutes.
    Timekeeper: Keeps track of time limitations.
```

Figure 3-5. Meeting roles chart for SELF-MANAGEMENT.

a. The *Leader* facilitates the meeting, using different participative processes to accomplish each agenda item. The Leader usually takes a leadership role in planning the meeting as well.

The manager or group leader does not have to lead the meeting. In fact, it is a good idea to rotate this responsibility. Be sure to assign responsibilities for the next meeting before your current meeting ends.

b. The *Recorder* records the group's comments, ideas, and decisions on chart paper.

Often the facilitator acts as the Recorder. But when the group is large or the conversation is difficult to facilitate, it is better to have a separate recorder. Give Recorders "spelling amnesty." Correct spelling is not critical, but it is important that Recorders capture the thoughts of all members of the group.

c. The *Minute Taker* prepares the minutes of the meeting.

The minutes of the meeting should include highlights of the discussions, the decisions made, and agreed-upon next steps.

d. The *Timekeeper* keeps track of the time limitations. (See VERBAL WARNINGS, Technique 6, for Timekeeper instructions.)

3. <u>When your meetings utilize small group discussions, each group should have a Timekeeper, Recorder, and Reporter.</u> The Timekeeper keeps track of the time limitations. The Recorder leads the small group discussion and records the group's comments, ideas, and decisions. The Reporter summarizes the results of small group discussions to the larger group when the groups reconvene. Have each group select its own facilitator for these roles.

Encourage groups to rotate responsibilities. Often groups will decide that the Recorder and the Reporter are the same person. This is acceptable as long as the group agrees and leadership rotates from time to time.

It is a good idea to move around and listen to what is happening within the groups, to assure that everyone's thoughts are documented and that everyone has a chance to be heard.

11

GO/NO GO

What is the easiest way to ascertain if our meeting group is ready to move to the next agenda item, or next part of our current discussion? Sometimes I'm not sure.

What is GO/NO GO?

GO/NO GO is a productivity technique to help your meeting group to decide whether or not to move forward. This can relate to the next agenda item, the next section of a complex question, the next step, the next question, or to any decision requiring a yes or no vote.

If an ongoing discussion is incomplete, as often occurs with complex issues, moving forward prematurely slows down or even undermines success. The GO/NO GO technique involves a simple voting procedure to make this determination.

When do I use GO/NO GO?

- When you want agreement from the group that it is time to move on.
- When you need agreement from the group to do something.

How do I use GO/NO GO?

1. <u>When you feel that it is time for the group to move on, take a vote.</u>
   You might say to the group, *"All in favor of moving forward to the next section/agenda item say GO. All in favor of not moving forward say NO GO."*

2. <u>When there are NO GO votes, address the concerns of the negative voters before moving forward.</u> Ask, *"What needs to happen before you will feel comfortable moving forward?"* Examples of NO GO reasons include a need to explore a fact further or gather additional information. Address NO GO issues in the appropriate manner.

3. <u>Revote as necessary.</u>

12

CHARTING

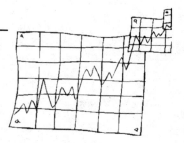

Even though I think my instructions are clear, participants frequently ask me to repeat what I say. Also, points that are made in the meeting are often repeated later on. This is frustrating and always seems to slow us down. Can you suggest a technique that will cure these problems?

What is CHARTING?

CHARTING is a productivity technique for increasing the effectiveness of communication in your meetings. This is accomplished by using visual aids to support your efforts.

Because so many studies show the accuracy of communication to be very low, it is important to use meeting facilitation techniques that sustain and reinforce the accuracy of memory. Many people are visual learners and they will concentrate better and remember much more when you use visual aids.

CHARTING significantly improves the accuracy of your communication, whether it be instructions, agendas, questions, data collection, discussions, or presentations.

When do I use CHARTING?

- When you want to improve the accuracy of communication in your meetings.
- When a point will be clearer with visual support.
- When giving instructions or directions.
- When there are many steps or key points to the facilitator's instructions or participants' comments.

How do I use CHARTING?

There are generally five types of information that use CHARTING in meetings. These are: Agendas and Ground Rules, Discussion Questions, Small Group and Individual Exercise Instructions, Discussion Points, and Decisions and Actions.

Agendas and ground rules. Chart and post your Agenda and Ground Rules where they can be seen throughout the meeting.

> Note: As you proceed through your agenda, check off where you are on the chart. This helps people to know where they are and where they're going. It gives them a sense of accomplishment. Refer back to your charted agenda from time to time, summarizing what has happened and what will happen.

Discussion questions. Post Discussion Questions on either an overhead or chart to help keep your group on track. See SHREDDED QUESTIONS, Technique 9, for specific ideas.

Small group and individual exercise instructions. During Small Group and Individual Exercises, chart and post all instructions and time frames.

> *Note:* These instructions should be prepared before the meeting on either charts or overheads. Overheads usually work better with larger groups. They are more easily read at a distance and from different positions in the room. Charts are better for smaller groups or when the information needs to be seen throughout the meeting. On rare occasions it is better to use both.

- Break instructions down into logical steps.
- Write legibly and as large as possible to ensure that everyone can read what you write.
- Use diverse colors.
- State time frames (e.g., 10 minutes) and finishing times (e.g., 9:25) for each of the steps.

Discussion points. Use chart paper to record discussions about all agenda items. This keeps conversations from going around in circles, keeps the same points from being repeated, and provides excellent data from which to prepare the minutes of your meeting.

> *Note:* Have small groups record their discussions on chart paper for their report back to the rest of the groups. This will also keep them from repeating themselves and help them keep on track. This is especially critical during brainstorming sessions.

> *Note:* See SELF-MANAGEMENT, Technique 10, for more on the role of the recorder in small group discussions.

Decisions and actions. Record all group decisions and actions or next steps on charts for inclusion in the minutes of the meeting.

13

ART

My participants sometimes seem to get bogged down in their own logic. This inhibits their creativity and negatively impacts the energy of the group. I am looking for a way to get people to think more creatively so we can develop a deeper understanding of an issue. Is there a technique that will help us see things through different eyes?

What is ART?

ART is a technique for helping your meeting participants to think and express themselves differently.

When people articulate their thoughts in atypical ways they tend to produce a wider spectrum of information. Sometimes the most unlikely methods of expression produce the most revealing information. This is because people are encouraged to use a different part of their brain, a part which taps and stimulates their perception differently.

ART involves having participants express their thoughts and ideas visually on paper. If used correctly, this type of artistic expression will increase the effectiveness of your meetings by providing new insights and increasing creativity, energy, and fun.

When do I use ART?

- When people need to visualize their future, a change, or a decision.
- When you want to clarify a point that is difficult to articulate.
- When you want to summarize what has been completed.
- When you want more creative input.

How do I use ART?

1. As a part of one or more relevant agenda items, <u>ask your participants to draw or otherwise visually depict their ideas on paper.</u>
   This can be done individually or in small groups, and the ART can be literal or figurative. Provide the necessary paper and a wide variety of colored markers.

   Option: You may also bring other art materials such as scissors, magazines to cut up, colored paper, and whatever else comes to mind.

   Note: Be sure that your instructions highlight that expression of ideas is the goal of the exercise. Artistic skill is irrelevant.

Note: You may perceive ART as a high-risk idea and thus be hesitant to use it. But try it! The technique works very well on all levels of an organization and can provide very creative and revealing information. You will be impressed with its effectiveness and high fun factor.

Following are some specific examples of how to initiate ART.

- To share information on staff responsibilities, you might say,

  Create a visual aid to explain how you spend your time in a typical week.

  Option: Use collages. Ask people to prepare a visual of the things they accomplished in the last year, e.g., pie charts of percentages of time use or projects accomplished.

- To gain an understanding of the group's current situation, say, for example,

  Draw a picture of what it feels like to work here.

- To create a vision of the group's preferred future, you could say,

  Imagine that we have been able to accomplish all we discussed and agreed on today. Think of our group in five years. (or another number based on your circumstances). *What will it look like?* Or you might say, *Draw an animal that describes our group as it is today. Draw another animal that describes the perfect group of the future.*

  Note: Use this information to create a list of words that describe your group's preferred future.

  Or, for example,

  Let's summarize our conclusions of the day. But instead of doing so verbally, tell us visually. If we do all the things we have agreed to today, what will the future look like?

- To gain information on the attitudes in your department, you might say,

  Show us, either literally or figuratively, what the attitude is in our department regarding the new management philosophy.

2. After the ART work is completed (usually 15 minutes is enough) follow with a short "report back" session, where the "artists" present and explain their work.

   Note: Keep the drawings and include them in the minutes of the meeting.

3. Ask the group to summarize what they learned from the ART process. For example, you might ask,

   What in particular stood out to you during this last exercise? What conclusions can we draw?

14

ANALOGIES AND METAPHORS

Analogy — a comparison that points out the similarity between the features of two different things.

Metaphor — a representation or a figurative expression for something.

Sometimes critical information isn't understood in our meetings as clearly as I would like. Important points seem to get lost because they are either complicated, dull, or both. What alternative methods do we have to get key points across?

What is ANALOGIES AND METAPHORS?

ANALOGIES AND METAPHORS is a technique to help your meeting participants focus and crystallize their thinking and understanding of an issue. It can also be used to emphasize key points of a topic under discussion. This technique is especially applicable for information that is difficult to understand or explain in simple terms. ANALOGIES AND METAPHORS involves using analogies and metaphors to explain and clarify the meaning of a specific issue. In addition to this primary goal, it can also help people to learn and think in new ways.

An analogy is a comparison that points out the similarity between the features of two different things. For example, one could make an analogy between a heart and a pump, or between a brain and a computer.

In a business setting, one might use the following analogy:

It is very difficult to explain our new IZUMA-RP222 computer chip, but it functions very much like the roundhouse of an old train station. Instead of having to go the long way around, the rotating track of the roundhouse provides a direct link to its destination. Our new chip provides this direct link and cuts the processing time exponentially.

A metaphor is a representation or a figurative expression for something. It is the application of a word or phrase to an object or concept it does not literally mean, in order to suggest comparison with another object or concept. In poetry, for example, a rose is often a metaphor for love, the rising sun is a metaphor for birth, and the waning moon is a metaphor for death.

In a business meeting, one could use this metaphor:

Our new environment technology will redefine our image to the extent that our factory stacks will seem like flower pots.

The ANALOGIES AND METAPHORS technique can be used as a communication strategy by the facilitator or as an exercise for the participants.

When do I use ANALOGIES AND METAPHORS?

- When a key point is difficult to understand on its own.
- When you want to make a point or explain something in a different way.
- When you want to emphasize a point.
- When you want to express personal perspectives in an impersonal but powerful way.

How do I use ANALOGIES AND METAPHORS?

AS A COMMUNICATION STRATEGY BEFORE THE MEETING

1. Identify the point you want to emphasize or explain.
2. Think of your audience. What is important to your audience? What can they relate to? Football, skiing, computers, food?
3. Brainstorm possible analogies and metaphors for use in the meeting.
4. Choose one or two of the best to use in your meeting.

AS A COMMUNICATION STRATEGY IN THE MEETING

Use the ANALOGIES AND METAPHORS as planned.

Note: It is a good idea to continually look for and think about effective ways to communicate ideas during your meetings. Tune in to your participants, improvise, and react with creative ideas as the situation presents itself.

AS AN EXERCISE FOR MEETING PARTICIPANTS

1. Introduce the topic and the ANALOGIES AND METAPHORS technique. Explain why you are asking the group to create these ANALOGIES AND METAPHORS and how they will be used. For example:

   Our primary supplier has asked us for feedback on working with them, and I'm meeting with their president on Thursday. As you know, he sometimes has a difficult time relating to our specific needs, so I thought it would be helpful if I could use a few analogies or metaphors in our meeting. I'd like your help in coming up with some ideas.

   Note: Other situations where you might use this technique include: sharing information among participants about a project or their jobs; exploring how it feels to work in a particular group or with a specific customer.

2. Ask the group to think silently for five minutes about ANALOGIES AND METAPHORS on a specific subject. Present an overview of the meaning of the two terms with a few examples on a chart or overhead, as in Fig. 3-6.
3. Ask your participants to share their best analogies and metaphors with the group. This can be either in small groups or as a large group.
4. Ask the group what can be concluded from the information. For example, *What points stuck out in your minds? What conclusions can we draw?*

CREATE AN ANALOGY OR METAPHOR TO DESCRIBE XX:

Spend five minutes thinking silently and individually about xx. What analogies or metaphors come to mind?

Analogy = a comparison that points out the similarity between the features of two different things. One can make an analogy between a heart and a pump, or a computer and a brain.

Metaphor = A representation or figurative expression. The application of a word or phrase to an object or concept it does not literally mean, in order to suggest comparison with another object or concept. A rose is often a metaphor for love, the rising sun for birth.

Figure 3-6. Instructions chart for ANALOGIES AND METAPHORS.

Option: If appropriate for the goals of the agenda item, have the group pick one or two of their analogies or metaphors that best summarize how they feel.

15

BREAKS

We seem to run out of steam long before our work has been completed. Do you have any ideas?

What is BREAKS?

BREAKS is a technique designed to support high energy and focus throughout your meeting.

Meetings are notorious for pushing on too long. The energy level of the group lowers as the meeting progresses and concentration and creativity suffer as a result. This problem is especially common when participative meeting techniques are not utilized. Research shows that people work better for longer periods of time when they are able to take short and frequent BREAKS. These BREAKS, five or ten minutes an hour, are far more beneficial than less frequent, longer BREAKS.

BREAKS give the group time to stretch and discuss the agenda informally. The facilitator can use BREAKS to ask for informal feedback on the meeting's processes and results, and prepare for the next items on the agenda.

When do I use BREAKS?

- When your meetings run more than one hour.
- When the group is stalled.
- When the group is in conflict and needs a few minutes to cool down.
- When you need time to regroup your thoughts; for example, if things are going badly.
- When you see or feel the group's energy waning.

How do I use BREAKS?

- Schedule BREAKS for longer meetings, and take unplanned BREAKS, with approval from the group, when appropriate.
- Use BREAKS to ask for feedback informally from your participants. Ask open-ended questions like, *"What are your reactions to the work we've done so far?"* This information will help you modify the agenda and processes if necessary.
- This is also a good time to talk with people who tend to be antagonistic or disruptive in the meeting. Often meeting facilitators will try to avoid these people, perceiving them as problems. Instead, use BREAKS to ask those people individually for their input. For example: To a person that seems to be resistant to the agenda, you could say, *"Tell me more about your concerns about the meeting today."*

You might learn valuable information and, at the very least, you will align your-self with them by showing sensitivity for their concerns.

■ Breaks are excellent opportunities to <u>talk to the person who has been dominating the meeting discussions.</u> You might say, *"I would like your help. I know that you feel very comfortable sharing your ideas and opinions, but not everyone in the group feels as comfortable as you. It's very important for us to hear everybody's ideas. I was wondering if you would help me do this by holding your ideas a few minutes until we have heard from the others. If your points of view haven't been stated by the others, then give us your ideas. What do you think? How would that work for you?"*

■ This is a great time to <u>deal with a situation involving conflict within a small number of group participants.</u> You can say in this situation, *"I know this issue is important to both of you, but I wonder if this meeting is the best place to resolve it. It seems that it doesn't include everyone, so I don't think it's a good use of everyone's time. What do you think?"*

■ Use this time to <u>prepare for the next agenda items.</u> Move charts, rearrange tables, etc.

Note: Remember to post the time (to the minute) when the meeting will reconvene. It is critical to start on time after your breaks. If you don't, you and your meetings lose credibility and momentum.

Note: If your meeting is exceedingly dull, BREAKS is not going to be enough to perk it up. You should look for other techniques to support your goals. Review the other techniques in this section for ideas. Don't hesitate to ask the group for their help if you are unsure about how to address the problem of a boring, unproductive meeting.

Option: Consider adding a short break to the end of small group exercises. This gives the slower groups time to catch up, while allowing the others time to rest officially.

16

MOVEMENT

What other techniques can I use to keep people alert and involved in our meetings?

What is MOVEMENT?

MOVEMENT is another technique designed to keep energy high and attention focused. Any purposeful MOVEMENT can reenergize your group, while at the same time supporting your meeting objectives.

When do I use MOVEMENT?

- When your meetings last more than a few hours.
- When you want to encourage participants to talk with new people.
- When you anticipate that the group's energy level will deteriorate, such as after lunch.
- When the group appears to be physically uncomfortable.

How do I use MOVEMENT?

1. <u>Periodically encourage participants to sit in different places, next to different people.</u> These changes can take place after BREAKS and are especially important if your meeting lasts through both the morning and the afternoon.

    Option: For small group discussions, have people consistently move to different parts of the room so that they interact with different people. This tends to be mentally stimulating and discourages the formation of cliques and alliances. This MOVEMENT also informally builds teamwork. This is most commonly done in one of two ways:

    a. Create predetermined discussion groups. Cluster participants with the maximum diversity of position, level within the organization, longevity on the job, and general perspective. Plan these groups, perhaps with the help of other participants, before the meeting.

    b. Create subgroups by asking participants to "number off." See SMALL GROUPS, Technique 20, for details.

2. <u>Use a light ball during round-robin exercises to keep the group active.</u>

    a. Explain the procedure. For example: *"The person who has the ball is the one who speaks. When that person is finished speaking, they will throw the ball to someone else, anyone they choose who has not yet spoken. Make sure that the ball gets around to everyone, thus giving everyone a chance to speak.*

b. Arbitrarily toss the ball to someone, asking him or her to start. Or, ask another person to choose who should start by throwing the ball to someone. Unless you are an outside facilitator, you should also speak on the subject.

c. When everyone has spoken, summarize and move on with your agenda.

3. <u>Ask participants to physically move to cluster around wall charts</u> used during specific components of your agenda.

17

TOYS

After an hour or so I start to see the signs. People start to fidget, they seem uncomfortable, and they lose concentration. We take frequent BREAKS and use MOVEMENT in our meetings as well, but I'd like to learn another alternative for getting active people to sit still long enough to listen and participate for extended periods of time.

What is TOYS?

TOYS is another technique designed to keep people focused and attentive for long periods of time.

"Sit still and pay attention!" This strict rule of behavior was taught to many of us as children, but it isn't helpful advice for everybody. Not all people listen better when they are sitting still and at attention. In fact, some listen much better and for longer periods of time when they can do something with their hands. TOYS is an uncomplicated and effective technique that involves allowing meeting participants to play with quiet toys during the meeting.

TOYS is not designed to replace BREAKS, Technique 15, or MOVEMENT, Technique 16, but to work with them in concert to help keep your participants relaxed, comfortable, attentive, involved, and productive.

When do I use TOYS?

- When people must sit and concentrate for long lengths of time.
- When your meeting participants rarely sit as part of their job.
- When you want to introduce an element of fun into your otherwise serious meetings.

How do I use TOYS?

BEFORE THE MEETING

1. Go to your local toy store and <u>purchase some simple toys.</u> The cost will be minimal. Buy only toys that won't require any mental concentration, make noise, or distract others in the group.

   Examples of excellent toys are:

   - Cush balls
   - Silly Putty
   - Colored pens and paper for doodling
   - Magnet toys
   - Finger puppets
   - Play-Doh

Note: Don't be afraid to try this technique with "serious" or upper level groups. They may need TOYS the most!

2. Randomly <u>place your TOYS on the tables</u> as you prepare the room for your meeting. If the tables are large, be sure that some TOYS will be within easy reach of everybody who will attend the meeting.

IN THE MEETING

1. As your meeting begins, <u>explain that the TOYS are there purposely for partici-pants to play with during the meeting.</u> Emphasize that this activity can occur at any time and without permission, but is an individual exercise. People who choose to use TOYS shouldn't distract others' thinking or participation. This tech-nique can be linked to the ground rule "fun is allowed." See GROUND RULES, Tech-nique 3, for details.

2. At the meeting's end, <u>ask participants to leave the TOYS for the next meeting</u> (unless you want to give them away as mementos).

Note: The first time you use TOYS in your meeting, ask for reactions from your meeting participants at the end of the meeting.

18

MUSIC

Sometimes I think that the energy swings in my meetings are due to the lack of diversity in my facilitation. And this sameness becomes a source of tedium for my participants. What can I do to change the atmosphere and the pace, or to create a different mood in my meetings?

What is MUSIC?

MUSIC is another technique designed to keep your meeting group's energy high.

MUSIC can set the stage for increased creativity and productivity by a simple change of mood. Well-planned MUSIC alters the ambience and tone of a meeting, thereby changing its pace and sparking the interest and attention of your participants. This reenergizes your group and provides an atmosphere that helps participants remain productive and mentally refreshed over long periods of time.

Make no mistake! MUSIC can be a very powerful tool in your meetings.

When do I use MUSIC?

- When you want to change the atmosphere to help you reinforce a point.
- When you want people to relax and focus on your meeting.
- When you want to emphasize a theme or point.
- When you want to review material in a different way.

How do I use MUSIC?

Use MUSIC before the meeting and during breaks.

BEFORE THE MEETING

Select music that will suit your audience and support the mood you want to create.

Note: Prepare to bring a portable CD or cassette player to the meeting.

Note: Instrumental music tends to be better because lyrics tend to distract conversations and thoughts.

IN THE MEETING

1. Turn the music on as you are setting up for the meeting, and as each break begins.
2. When the music stops, it signifies that the meeting is ready to begin.

Use MUSIC to introduce, emphasize, or reinforce a point or issue.

BEFORE THE MEETING

1. Select a piece of lyrical or instrumental music that literally or emotionally underscores a planned agenda item or piece of information.

2. If possible, bring a broad selection of MUSIC with you to your meetings. This is so you will be able to improvise with this technique as the situation presents itself. Music can help to cool tempers, negate conflict, introduce humor, stimulate optimism, and awaken creativity.

IN THE MEETING

Play the MUSIC during the appropriate part of your agenda.

Option: Let the participants select or create a "theme song" for a specific project or for their group. They may want to alter the words to an existing song to suit their purposes.

Use MUSIC along with visual aids as a review or meeting summary. This can be done at the completion of a section of the agenda, at the end of the day, or at the beginning of a subsequent day.

BEFORE THE MEETING

1. Select a piece of MUSIC that will be generally pleasing to your audience and appropriate for your review.

2. Sequentially prepare the visual aids, such as charts, graphs, slides, and overheads, that you will use in the review.

3. Decide if you should present this material to the group or if your meeting participants should independently review the material.

Note: If you choose to present the material, decide if you will do so nonverbally, or present the review in "rap" style, verbally reviewing the material synchronized with the music.

4. Decide how best to display your visual aids. These can be displayed throughout the room, or from the front of the room.

5. Practice with the actual music you will use during your meeting, whether your presentation will be nonverbal or verbal.

IN THE MEETING

1. Prepare the group for the summary. You might say, for example:

We are going to review the highlights of yesterday's planning meeting using music as a backdrop. This review will remind us where we left off, and prepare us for our next agenda item where we will prioritize the decisions we made.

2. Start the music and begin your review, using your overheads, charts, and other graphics. Present the material in a way that leads your participants through the information you are reviewing.

Note: Remember to keep it quick and simple. Let the MUSIC and visuals speak for themselves. On the other hand, use your imagination and have some fun.

3. Turn off the MUSIC when the summary is completed.

19

WRITING

I know that meetings are designed for two-way communication, but sometimes a verbal discussion doesn't seem the best way to utilize the time of my meeting participants. This usually happens when the agenda is long, the group is large, only a few people participate, or the information requested is delicate or volatile. Is there an alternative technique to group discussions?

What is WRITING?

WRITING is a productivity technique designed to increase individual participation. This process involves obtaining specific and thoughtful written information from all participants before or instead of a verbal discussion.

Many people prefer to think before they speak. Others need time to formulate their ideas, especially concerning complex issues. Allowing a short time for quiet contemplation combined with asking participants to write their comments down on paper increases individual input and the number and variety of ideas. This technique not only meets the needs of these participants, but also is the fastest, most efficient method of gathering information.

WRITING can also be used before the meeting to gather specified information from the group. This can further improve time spent in the meeting itself.

When do I use WRITING?

- When you need to brainstorm or gather information quickly.
- When participants are uncomfortable speaking in front of a group.
- When some participants in the group tend to dominate conversations.
- When you want to collect information before the meeting.
- When information must be exchanged but face-to-face dialogue is not necessary.

How do I use WRITING?

BEFORE THE MEETING

1. Consider WRITING as a technique as you plan the details of your agenda. Some specific options follow:

   As a brainstorming technique:

   - CARD CLUSTERS, Technique 31

As a technique for gathering premeeting information:

- QUESTIONNAIRES, Technique 37

As a technique for gathering information on individual perspectives on a problem:

- NOMINAL GROUP PROCESS, Technique 43

As a technique for gathering personal perspectives about how a group has worked together:

- PROUDS AND SORRIES, Technique 46
- KEEP/THROW, Technique 47

As a technique for evaluating the meeting:

- WRITTEN QUESTIONS, Technique 72

2. Purchase and prepare the necessary supplies. This includes an adequate number of sticky notes (or cards and tape) and felt-tip pens.

IN THE MEETING

Use the information as planned.

20

SMALL GROUPS

Sometimes it seems impossible to hear from everyone in our meetings. The group is too large, the agenda is too long, or the time is too short. How can I be sure that all members get a chance to speak their minds?

What is SMALL GROUPS?

SMALL GROUPS is a productivity technique for gaining input from everyone in the meeting. This process involves breaking a large group into smaller, more manageable groups of participants.

SMALL GROUPS stimulates fuller participation, requires less time, and tends to create higher energy and better results. It can be combined with WRITING, Technique 19, to create a thoughtful and participative discussion.

When do I use SMALL GROUPS?

- When your meeting involves more than five people.
- When some participants are uncomfortable speaking in front of groups of people.
- When an issue requires in-depth discussion.
- When you want to increase participation without increasing time commitments.

How do I use SMALL GROUPS?

BEFORE THE MEETING

1. When creating the agenda, <u>determine if and when SMALL GROUPS is the best technique</u> to use in specific parts of your meeting.

2. <u>Determine the questions you want each SMALL GROUP to address.</u>

   Note: See SHREDDED QUESTIONS, Technique 9, or OPEN-ENDED QUESTIONS, Technique 34, for ideas.

3. <u>Determine how best to create the SMALL GROUPS.</u> SMALL GROUPS of three to six people are ideal.

   Option A: Ask participants to "number off" in your meeting. For example, if your group includes 35 people, create seven groups of five people each. Ask participants to "number off" from one to seven to create these groups.

   Option B: Ask the participants to cluster with two or three people sitting near them. You might want to help form these SMALL GROUPS to avoid anyone being left without a group, or unevenly distributed groups.

Note: This option is particularly effective if participants do not know each other yet, or if your meeting has just started and there is no present need for MOVEMENT, Technique 16, at this time.

Option C: Create lists of SMALL GROUPS before the meeting, usually working for maximum diversity within each group. There may be times when you want groups based by region, level in the organization, or intact work groups. But generally, maximum diversity gives groups a broader outlook and creates a sense of team across traditional boundaries. If the meeting calls for several SMALL GROUP discussions, you can create several lists (for example, groups for agenda item 1, groups for agenda item 2, etc.). Post these lists and give copies to all participants. This will avoid confusion whenever new SMALL GROUPS form.

Option D: When your group has a long history together and seems tired of these other options, ask them to break into groups in nontraditional ways, for instance, by birthday. For example, *"All those born in the first quarter of the year (January, February, and March) form a group in this corner of the room."*

Note: This can also help informally create rapport among the group. Give them a few minutes to share birthdays before starting their official tasks. Before the report back, ask if anyone shares a birthday with another participant, or if anyone has a birthday that day.

This technique can be modified as you wish. Create SMALL GROUPS based on anything that would work for the group. Use your imagination and make it fun.

4. Plan and prepare specific instructions for each SMALL GROUP exercise. Include SELF-MANAGEMENT instructions, Technique 10. Create visual aids to help the groups stay on track. See CHARTING, Technique 12, for details.

Option: All groups answer the same questions.

Option: All groups answer different questions.

Option: A few groups answer one question while other groups answer a different question.

Note: Determine whether to ask the same or different questions based on the number of questions that need to be answered and the relative importance of each question to the goals of the agenda item.

5. Plan how SMALL GROUPS will report back their ideas to the larger group. Report back options include:

a. Each SMALL GROUP reports back their best one or two ideas using a chart or overhead as a visual aid.

b. Each SMALL GROUP reports back their suggested next steps. Consider a combination of (a) and (b) as another option.

c. Each SMALL GROUP reports back a concise summary of their discussion using chart paper or overhead as a visual aid.

d. All SMALL GROUP reports are written on chart paper for all participants to read during a break.

e. Each SMALL GROUP has its work reproduced and distributed to all participants.

f. Give SMALL GROUP reports to a special summarizing group, which prepares a concise written or verbal summary.

g. Use other visual aids in your reports, such as collages or pictures. See ART, Technique 13, for further information.

6. Decide how all the information created by the SMALL GROUPS will be used.

DURING THE MEETING

1. Explain the purpose and process of the SMALL GROUPS technique.

2. Break the large group into SMALL GROUPS and give them their specific instructions.

3. Each SMALL GROUP discusses and reports back on the specific topic under consideration.

4. Use the resulting information as planned.

4

7 Techniques to Boost Creativity and Teamwork

Miguel is part of a new self-directed work team. The team is an experiment and some managers within the organization are skeptical about the idea.

Helping to get this department out of the mess it's in is going to be a lot of work. And it's going to take a lot more than a single jump start to keep things moving in the right direction. We know that we need to change our old mind-set, but we're not exactly sure how to go about doing it.

New and creative ideas are essential to any organization's future competitiveness. The rules and ideas that defined organizational success in the past no longer apply. Old models and ideas simply don't provide suitable answers to the complex and multifaceted demands of the new world.

Teamwork is just as critical as creativity. The nature of work has become too interdependent for one person or a small group of unconnected people to effectively address complex organizational issues. The better a group works together, the more efficient and successful they become.

This chapter describes seven techniques that stimulate the creativity and teamwork that are essential to every successful participative meeting. These techniques are:

- 21 THINKING OUT OF THE BOX
- 22 NEW GLASSES
- 23 INCREDIBALLS
- 24 TEAM LEARNING

- 25 TWO TRUTHS AND A LIE
- 26 MILESTONES
- 27 THE FUNERAL

21

THINKING OUT OF THE BOX

One of my meeting groups is very analytical and established in the way they deal with each other and with the problems they face. This group definitely needs a push to help them start thinking in new ways. Do you have any ideas?

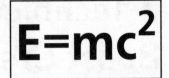

What is THINKING OUT OF THE BOX?

THINKING OUT OF THE BOX is a technique designed to help your participants see the value of thinking in new and different ways.

People think and solve problems within their personal paradigms. Paradigms are the sets of beliefs each of us hold that structure our thinking and the ways in which we view the world. When we resist challenging our paradigms, we restrict our ability to perceive a fuller picture of the world, and thereby limit our ability to excel. Problem solving is an especially creative process, and THINKING OUT OF THE BOX is an exercise that can help people to open their concepts and methods of perception and analysis.

When do I use THINKING OUT OF THE BOX?

- When your group seems to be stuck.
- When you know the group's thinking will need to be challenged in order to effectively solve a problem or be more competitive.
- When your group needs to look at things in different ways.

How do I use THINKING OUT OF THE BOX?

BEFORE THE MEETING

1. Determine how you want to use and introduce THINKING OUT OF THE BOX.
2. Create an overhead or chart as shown in Fig. 4-1.

DURING THE MEETING

1. Introduce the exercise. You might say, for example,

   This next agenda item is going to take some creative thinking. To get us warmed up, let's do a quick exercise.

   Note: When you introduce and explain the exercise, don't use the words "thinking out of the box," as that would provide too obvious a hint for the solution to the puzzle. Use the words "Nine Dot Exercise" instead.

NINE DOT EXERCISE

Connect all the dots using no more than four straight lines, and without retracing your steps.

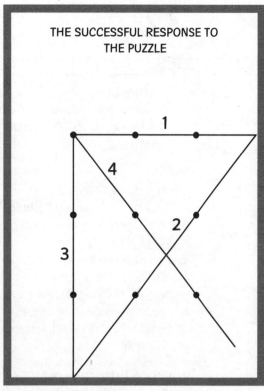

THE SUCCESSFUL RESPONSE TO THE PUZZLE

Figure 4-1. Instructions for the Nine Dot Exercise.

Figure 4-2. The successfully completed Nine Dot Exercise.

2. Explain the exercise with the help of your chart or overhead. Ask participants to solve the puzzle individually.

3. Demonstrate how to solve the puzzle. After a few minutes, ask if anyone has solved the problem. Invite one person who has solved the puzzle (be sure to verify that they have done so successfully first) to come forward to demonstrate how the puzzle can be solved.

   Note: If no one has solved the puzzle, complete it yourself on the chart or overhead.

4. Debrief the exercise by asking the following questions:

   What made it difficult to THINK OUTSIDE THE BOX? What is the value of THINKING OUT OF THE BOX for us here today? What are the dangers of THINKING OUT OF THE BOX? How can we remind ourselves to THINK OUT OF THE BOX?

   Note: This exercise is very popular. If it is well-known within your participant group, use the THINKING OUT OF THE BOX terminology as a quick reminder. It may still be worthwhile to use the Nine Dot model as a visual reminder from time to time.

22

NEW GLASSES

Some of my group's participants seem resistant to change and insist on looking at problems in the same old ways. Is there a simple technique that can help them snap out of their old habits and perceptions?

What is NEW GLASSES?

NEW GLASSES is a simple technique to help your meeting participants look at the meeting agenda's topics through "new eyes," supporting them in leaving their biases and old perspectives behind. It is an instantaneous energizer and also serves as a good learning tool for the tactile learner.

NEW GLASSES involves literally putting on a pair of silly glasses when old style or habitual thinking patterns are exposed. The absurdity of this technique allows people to step outside themselves and look at the world through "new eyes." Don't be afraid to try it! NEW GLASSES works and everybody has fun with it.

When do I use NEW GLASSES?

- When participants have preconceived ideas about agenda topics.
- When you lead a strategic planning, reengineering, or any other type of meeting where changes will be made.

How do I use NEW GLASSES?

BEFORE THE MEETING

Buy each participant in your meeting group a pair of silly glasses. These can be purchased at a costume shop or children's toy store. Buy several varieties and wrap them up as presents.

DURING THE MEETING

1. Hand out the presents to all participants.

Option A: Distribute the presents after your group agrees on the meeting ground rules (see GROUND RULES, Technique 3), especially if you have a ground rule for "thinking with an open mind."

Option B: Distribute the presents at any point during the meeting when the group will be challenged to look at the world through "new eyes."

2. At the appropriate time, <u>ask the participants to open their presents and give them a try. Explain their purpose.</u> Tell them that the glasses are designed to help them look at the world through "new eyes." Explain that if, at any time during the meeting, the participants feel they are falling into old ways of looking at the world, they should put their glasses on. Or, if they think that any other person is falling into old habits and perspectives, they may ask that person to put on their glasses.

Note: The glasses also serve as another toy (see TOYS, Technique 17) to fiddle with during the meeting, and will usually be the source of needed humor periodically throughout the meeting.

23

INCREDIBALLS

More than ever before, our group needs to start making some radical improvements in the way we do our business. We haven't worked particularly well together in the past and I need to get these people together and jolted fast. Do you have any suggestions?

What is INCREDIBALLS?

INCREDIBALLS is a technique that motivates people to work together as a team and challenges them to think about ways to work together differently and more efficiently.

The INCREDIBALLS exercise presents increasingly difficult and seemingly impossible deadlines, which stimulates creative thinking and solutions. By using the INCREDIBALLS technique, the power and importance of both teamwork and creative thinking will be graphically displayed.

When do I use INCREDIBALLS?

- When your group is about to begin an improvement or reengineering project.
- When your group is stuck in the way they think and work together.

How do I use INCREDIBALLS?

BEFORE THE MEETING

1. Put INCREDIBALLS (or team exercise) on your agenda. Allow 30 to 40 minutes.

   Note: Your group must have more than five and fewer than thirty participants. If your group is very large, ask for a smaller group of volunteers. The rest of the group can act as observers.

2. Purchase three tennis balls and number the balls 1, 2, and 3 with a marker.

DURING THE MEETING

1. Set up the exercise:

   a. Explain the purpose of INCREDIBALLS. For example:

   This exercise is designed to help us look at how we work together, how we might want or need to work together in the future, and have some fun besides.

   b. Ask the INCREDIBALLS participants to move from their seats to stand in a circle.

     Note: This may mean moving tables and chairs aside, or moving to a different space large enough for the group to form a circle.

SOURCE: Organizational Development Department, Boeing Commercial Airplane Group.

Then you might say,

For the next 10 minutes you are no longer members of (the name of your organization here), *but of a newly formed organization. What should be the name of your new organization?* (Use the group's chosen new name for the rest of the exercise.) *Usually an organization would define its vision, mission, goal, and objectives before its organizational structure was created. But for purposes of this exercise we'll presume that the essential, preliminary work is completed, and jump right to your organizational structure.*

Note: Ask participants who are familiar with INCREDIBALLS to participate but not divulge their experience. Tell them that they can have extra fun by observing what happens this time compared to the other times they played. Participants who are familiar with the game can assist as the timekeeper and observer for you.

Option: If your group is larger than 30 people, ask for 15 to 20 volunteers to participate in INCREDIBALLS and for the others to be observers. Thirty is the preferred maximum number for INCREDIBALLS.

2. <u>Give the ball to someone (Mr. or Ms. X) in your group</u> who doesn't usually take a leadership role. Ask Mr. or Ms. X to throw the ball to someone else, who then throws it to someone else, in turn to someone else, etc. Ask the participants to remember who threw the ball to them and who they threw it to. The last person to receive the ball returns it to Mr. or Ms. X. <u>Give the group a practice run with one ball.</u>

Note: Groups usually make mistakes the first time, so let them get the sequence down with another practice session before going on.

3. Once they have completed the practice run without error, <u>explain that increased production requires that they triple their output and their efforts will now be timed. Explain the 3 requirements of the exercise.</u> Tell the group, for example,

Your organization is doing so well that demand for your product has tripled, but you have decided that your staffing levels will remain the same. So from now on you must work with all three balls. (Hold up the balls which you have numbered 1, 2, and 3.) *Not only that, but from now on, your customers will time your work. And finally, your customers have given you three simple requirements:*

- *You must maintain the same person-to-person sequence.*
- *The balls must be contacted in the order they are put into play.*
- *The process begins and ends with Mr. or Ms. X.*

Note: These requirements can also be posted.

Note: These requirements are designed to create perceived walls around what can and cannot be done. In reality, they are to be taken as three separate requirements and to be observed very creatively. In fact, they must be observed very creatively for the group to achieve its goal.

If your group asks you for clarification or approval, tell them

Your customers are not available at this time. They left only these three in-structions, and felt sure that your group would understand the require-ments correctly.

As they complete the exercise with three balls, time them.

Note: Ask Mr. or Ms. X to say *"start"* and *"stop"* to assist you in timing the group correctly.

Note: If you do not have a watch with a second hand, ask to borrow one from one of the participants.

4. <u>Begin the exercise and record the time.</u> Write the time on a nearby chart or board, and share the time verbally with the group. <u>Then explain that because their competitors have cut their production time in half, it is necessary for this group to do the same.</u> For example,

Your customers have just found a competitor who can produce the same product in half the time. They'd like to continue to work with you, but you must produce your product in at least the same time as your com-petitor. The customer requirements remain the same. You are allowed the time you need to discuss how you plan to accomplish the goal. Let me know when you are ready, and I will time your process again.

After the group completes its task, communicate and record the time.

5. <u>Repeat Step Four a few times, each time requiring that the time be cut in half until the time for completion of the exercise is down to under one second</u> (one second is not a misprint).

Note: If the group needs prodding during this part of the exercise, tell them that another group you worked with recently did the exercise in less than one second.

6. <u>When the group achieves the goal of one second,</u> ask them to give themselves a round of applause and go back to their seats.

7. <u>Debrief the experience as a group.</u> Customize questions based on your situa-tion. Here are sample debriefing questions:

How did you work together as a team? How well did you listen to all the ideas presented? What made reaching the goal difficult? What were your perceptions or assumptions about the customer requirements? How did those perceptions or assumptions hamper your ability to be success-ful? What allowed you to be successful in the end? How can we use this experience to improve our ability to work as a team in the future?

Note: If you had neutral observers, ask them what they observed about the way the group worked together. For example:

How well did the exercise participants listen to everyone's ideas? Did everyone offer ideas? How did the group decide what to do next?

24

TEAM LEARNING

Our group is limited to our own old habits, opinions, and experiences. But the challenges facing us call for a fuller understanding and broader perspective. We joke that we all need to go back to college to get some new ideas, but, of course, there's no time for that now. Do you have any suggestions?

What is TEAM LEARNING?

TEAM LEARNING is a technique that provides a work team with the resources and mechanisms to learn new information. Teams often become so busy doing things and making decisions that they don't take any time for the reflection, learning, and dialogue needed to stimulate new perspectives, insights, and wisdom. In addition to providing this new knowledge, TEAM LEARNING can be effectively employed as a forum for the group to share ideas, opinions, and controversial subjects.

TEAM LEARNING information can come from people, films, articles, or other resources, and can provide the missing link to effective long-term thinking and decision making.

When do I use TEAM LEARNING?

- When your group needs new skills, ideas, and perspectives to be successful.
- When it is necessary to introduce new or controversial information.
- When you want to build a sense of team as a by-product of learning.

How do I use TEAM LEARNING?

1. Introduce the technique and <u>discuss the need for TEAM LEARNING with the group.</u> You might start the conversation by saying,

   In order for us to work as effectively as we need to, it seems that we need to make a commitment to continuous learning. What do you think?

2. <u>Determine, with the help of the group, what TEAM LEARNING is needed and what methods should be used.</u>

   Option A: Find films that will provide useful information. Look for films on topics pertinent to the group's work, industry, or areas for skill development.

Note: Many metropolitan areas have business film rental and purchase services that will allow you to view films before rental or purchase. These services are also well informed about what films are available for your particular needs.

Option B: Books or articles from newspapers, professional journals, or other publications can also serve this purpose. Have your group read a periodical or book together, perhaps one chapter a week, and discuss it as an agenda item at your meetings. Some groups opt for weekly or monthly "brown bag" lunch discussions.

Option C: Using experts or other people from outside the group is another idea. These people could come from a local university, another organization, or another department or division within your own organization. Remember to consider those inside the group with special expertise as well.

Note: Experts do not necessarily come from high levels within their organizations. For example, the best experts may be those directly involved with the manufacture of a specific item. See CONTENT EXPERTS, Technique 45, for details on briefing outside experts.

Option D: Tours or field trips can also be very insightful. Consider touring the facilities of customers using your products. Visit a noncompeting firm to view their manufacturing facilities, office setup, or specific services. These tours can be used to gather new information, understand customer needs better, or benchmark "best practices."

3. Gain agreement on the purpose, methods, and scheduling of TEAM LEARNING. Ask for one or more volunteers to be responsible for coordinating activities. This responsibility could rotate. Document your agreements on chart paper and distribute as part of the minutes of your meeting.

4. Carry out the TEAM LEARNING as planned.

5. As part of each learning session, debrief or summarize the TEAM LEARNING information. Examples of debriefing questions include:

What were the key points that we learned? What was your reaction to what we heard today? What would be the positives for us? And the negatives? What alternatives to our present methods of working do we have? What action shall we take?

Use SHREDDED QUESTIONS, Technique 9, for additional ideas for your own situation.

Note: Debriefing the TEAM LEARNING information is critical. Without this important step, much of the energy and potential from the inclusion of this new information will be wasted.

25

TWO TRUTHS AND A LIE

Even though we've worked together for a while, no one seems to know very much about the other people in the group. Is there a fun and simple technique that will help us learn more about our fellow participants?

What is TWO TRUTHS AND A LIE?

TWO TRUTHS AND A LIE is a team-building exercise that provides your meeting participants with personal information that reveals more about the other team members as individuals. This information can help build a more intimate and productive relationship among people within your group.

By providing fun and revealing pieces of trivia about themselves, people tend to expose their humanity. This process generally allows people to work better together because of their fuller understanding of and compassion for their teammates.

When do I use TWO TRUTHS AND A LIE?

- When you want a quick, fun exercise to help build relationships among meeting participants.
- When you want to use a different form of introduction (see INTRODUCTIONS, Technique 1) with a group that has already worked together in the past.

How do I use TWO TRUTHS AND A LIE?

BEFORE THE MEETING

1. Put TWO TRUTHS AND A LIE on your agenda.

    Option: Depending on the size of your group, this can be used as a large or small group exercise.

    > *Note:* If you choose to use this technique in small groups, decide how to break up the groups ahead of time. (See SMALL GROUPS, Technique 20, for options.) Ask small groups to nominate one favorite example to share with the larger group.

2. Prepare a chart explaining the exercise, such as in Fig. 4-3.

DURING THE MEETING

1. Introduce TWO TRUTHS AND A LIE to the group and explain to the group how to prepare for the exercise, using a chart or overhead similar to Fig. 4-3 to reinforce the explanation.

TWO TRUTHS AND A LIE

1. Take a few minutes silently to think of TWO TRUTHS AND A LIE about yourself.
2. When everyone is prepared, we will all verbally share our TWO TRUTHS AND A LIE with the group.
3. After each presentation, the other members of the group will guess which statement is the lie.
4. You will then share with the group which of your statements is the lie.

Figure 4-3. Instructions for TWO TRUTHS AND A LIE.

Consider using yourself as an example. You might say, for example, *"I grew up on a pig farm with nine brothers and sisters, I was fired twice as a waitress, and I'm an avid downhill skier. Guess which one isn't true."*

Option: Ask managers in the group to share their TWO TRUTHS AND A LIE with the large group as a kick-off.

Note: Be sure to tell the managers ahead of time, so they will be prepared and will not need time to think in the meeting. This will use the other participants' time wisely.

2. Complete the exercise, giving each participant time to share their TWO TRUTHS AND A LIE. After a participant has shared three personal statements, ask the group to guess which is the lie. After a few moments of guessing, ask the participant to share which of the three statements was a lie. Then move on, until you have heard from each participant.

26

MILESTONES

I want a technique for helping our group to understand and appreciate the diversity of experience and backgrounds in the room, but in an informal and interesting way. Do you have any ideas?

What is MILESTONES?

MILESTONES is a technique that allows for participants to learn more about the members of their meeting group, thereby building a stronger sense of team. By focusing on MILESTONES in each participant's life, the exercise promotes learning more about each other, both on a personal and professional level, and ultimately helps people work together more effectively.

It is often an underlying goal of any meeting for participants to have the opportunity to get to know each other better. MILESTONES provides for this kind of information flow, quickly and informally.

When do I use MILESTONES?

- When you want to build a stronger sense of team.
- When you want your participants to learn more about each other's personal history and interests.
- When you need a productive break from a long and serious agenda.

How do I use MILESTONES?

BEFORE THE MEETING

1. Include MILESTONES on your agenda.

    Note: Allow about 15 minutes total for the exercise, and place MILESTONES on the agenda immediately before a break.

2. Create a MILESTONES chart using large butcher paper, or a few chart papers taped together. Create the chart with five-year interval markers, similar to Fig. 4-4, and be sure to leave enough room under each year for a number of sticky notes.

    Note: Decide how far back your MILESTONES chart should go by estimating the age of the oldest person in the group. If you aren't sure, create your chart based on the maximum age before retirement (for example, the year of your meeting minus 65 years).

3. Prepare an instructions chart for MILESTONES similar to Fig. 4-5.

DURING THE MEETING

1. Introduce the technique and explain the purpose of MILESTONES. You might say, for example:

MILESTONES

1935 1940 1945 1950 1955 1960 1965 1970 1975 1980 etc.

Figure 4-4. MILESTONES chart.

The purpose of this exercise is to share important information about our-selves. This is designed to help us all understand more about the back-grounds of the individuals on the team. Let's take the next 10 minutes to chart our personal MILESTONES.

2. Give instructions for MILESTONES, and support your explanation with a prepre-pared chart, as illustrated in Fig. 4-5.

   a. Using sticky notes, have your participants write three personal MILESTONES in their lives, one MILESTONE per sticky note. MILESTONES should be written in the third person, and can be funny or serious. Give some examples to your group. You might say, for example,

      Helen rode her bike across the country in 1975. Richard skied for the first time at age 40. After ten years of not so serious study at the uni-versity, Roger finally received his bachelor's degree in 1980.

      Note: If the group is small (fewer than 10 people), you may choose to have everyone provide four or five MILESTONES.

   b. After they're finished, have your participants place each MILESTONE sticky note on the MILESTONE chart under the appropriate year.

      Note: This exercise can also be used for sharing company, department, or work area MILESTONES.

   c. Encourage your participants to read the MILESTONE chart at their leisure, preferably during breaks or at lunch.

3. When everyone understands the instructions, complete the exercise.

MILESTONES INSTRUCTIONS

1. Think of three personal milestones in your life. Write one per sticky note. Write your milestones in the third person. For example: Amy was born on the first day of World War II.

2. As you leave for the break, place your sticky notes at the appropriate year on the chart provided.

3. During the break, read the MILESTONES of the others.

Figure 4-5. MILESTONES instructions.

27

THE FUNERAL

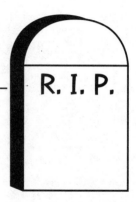

R. I. P.

Our group has just gone through downsizing and re-structuring, and we're having a difficult time letting go of the past. This negatively impacts our ability to concentrate on future demands. What can I do to help the group deal with this type of situation?

What is THE FUNERAL?

THE FUNERAL is a technique for helping a group put the past aside and prepare for the future. THE FUNERAL acknowledges in a good-natured way that the past had both its good points and its bad. But in order to go forward, the past must now be "buried" and the present and future must be embraced.

THE FUNERAL is exactly what it implies, but obviously in symbolic terms. Emotions are strong after a significant change. Giving some time to acknowledge the grieving of the group can be very healthy. Rituals, such as THE FUNERAL, create a rite of passage and can be a powerful tool in helping a group move forward.

When do I use THE FUNERAL?

- When the group is downsizing, being purchased, or is the subject of other significant cultural changes.
- When a dysfunctional group has agreed to act differently in the future.
- When a group can't seem to go forward because of a perceived loss of any kind.

How do I use THE FUNERAL?

VARIATION 1

1. Talk with your meeting group about what has happened (i.e., recent or upcoming downsizing, corporate takeover, etc.). Ask for their support in taking a few hours to acknowledge the changes in a ceremonious fashion. Note that the idea may seem a little silly but that it has been found to help groups work through their emotional energy about a change and feel more prepared to work together in the future. Explain that THE FUNERAL will be a time to remember the good and the bad, and to bury the past. At THE FUNERAL, everyone who wants to will have an opportunity to speak. They could prepare poems or short stories in writing, sing, or provide music if they wish. THE FUNERAL will literally be a mock funeral for the past.

2. Agree on a time and place to hold THE FUNERAL.

   Note: If planned during the workday, schedule this for the end of the day.

3. Ask for a few volunteers to plan the event.

4. Ask the participants to wear clothes they would wear for a funeral.

5. Together with your planning team, create an agenda for THE FUNERAL.

Incorporate the cultural traditions of people within your group. Either provide a coffin or "cremate" the past and spread the ashes. Poems, photographs, articles, et cetera can go in the coffin. Find a place to bury your coffin or spread the ashes. Provide beverages and food for the group, just as a gathering of friends and family would after the loss of a loved one.

6. Hold THE FUNERAL.

7. The next time your group meets after THE FUNERAL, take a few minutes at the meeting to ask for their reactions and comments.

VARIATION 2

Note: This variation is for a group that has worked together poorly in the past and has agreed to work together differently in the future.

1. Talk with the group to confirm agreement to work together differently in the future. Ask for their support in taking some time to ceremoniously let go of the past and prepare for the future.

2. Agree on a time and place for THE FUNERAL. THE FUNERAL ceremony should be the only agenda item.

3. Before that meeting, create a little mock coffin or other suitable symbol of passing. Provide paper and pencils for each participant.

4. Ask the participants to write on paper all the negative thoughts they have had about each other in the past, all their bad habits, et cetera. After they are finished, ask them to shred their papers and put them in the "coffin." They need not share any of their comments with the others.

5. When everyone has finished, close the "coffin" you have created.

6. Take the "coffin" to a predetermined place for burial or burning. As you are disposing of the coffin, ask for a moment of silence for all old habits and attitudes.

   Note: If you choose to burn the coffin, check for compliance with any open-air burning laws.

   Option: Put the coffin in the company box crusher and keep it somewhere in the department as a reminder that old ways of working together are no longer acceptable.

7. Bring THE FUNERAL to a close with music or by humming a song known to the group.

8. The next time the group meets, debrief the exercise.

5

6 Techniques to Brainstorm Ideas

Harold's accounting department was rock bottom on the division's customer satisfaction results for the third time in five years.

We're getting heat from every direction. And it seems that the harder we try, the worse it gets. Our brainstorming sessions go over like a lead balloon. Maybe we're too quick to criticize our ideas or just too anxious to make a decision and move on. But what can we do?

Every group within today's organizations is expected to provide creative solutions. They need to find better ways of doing business, as well as expose, analyze, and deal with problems before they even occur.

The best way to find the most effective idea is to first introduce as many ideas as possible. And that means brainstorming. Brainstorming is founded upon the principle that the quantity of ideas increases their quality. The first ideas are typically the most obvious. But when brainstormers are fearful of scrutiny and judgment during the brainstorming session, ideas stop flowing before the best ideas come forward. Deferring the judgment of ideas improves the volume of participant input and consequently the value.

This chapter provides six brainstorming techniques that are designed to guide the meeting facilitator toward improving the outcome of any organization's brainstorming efforts.

These techniques are:

- 28 THE OLD-FASHIONED WAY
- 29 MINDMAPPING
- 30 STORY BOARDING
- 31 CARD CLUSTERS
- 32 STP
- 33 BREAKING A STALEMATE

28

THE OLD-FASHIONED WAY

Sometimes I need to gather a lot of ideas quickly, especially when a large group of participants is involved. Is there a basic brainstorming technique that will function well under these circumstances?

What is THE OLD-FASHIONED WAY?

THE OLD-FASHIONED WAY is the original brainstorming technique. It is tried and true as a technique that enables participants to express significant amounts of information or ideas in a short period of time. THE OLD-FASHIONED WAY works well for both small and large groups.

The general rules for THE OLD-FASHIONED WAY serve as the basis or foundation for the other brainstorming techniques included in this chapter.

When do I use THE OLD-FASHIONED WAY?

- When you want to generate a large quantity of information before problem solving, decision making, or planning.
- When you want to inspire creativity and gather ideas.

How do I use THE OLD-FASHIONED WAY?

1. Introduce the topic and the purpose of the specific brainstorming session. Remind the group of the ground rules for brainstorming and consider posting these ground rules on a chart, as illustrated in Fig. 5-1.

BRAINSTORMING GROUND RULES

1. All ideas and information are acceptable.
2. No criticism or analysis of ideas or information is permitted.
3. Build on the ideas of others.
4. All ideas and information are charted.

Figure 5-1. Ground rules for BRAINSTORMING.

SOURCE: A.F. Osborn, *Applied Imagination* (Old Tappan, NJ: Scribner's, 1963).

2. Begin the discussion by asking a specific open-ended question to focus the discussion (see OPEN-ENDED QUESTIONS, Technique 34). For example:

What should we name our new product? What do we need to accomplish before the conference begins? What can we do to capture a larger market share?

Ask your participants to "popcorn" their ideas. ("Popcorn" means allowing participants to voice their ideas in an unorderly and unrestrained sequence.)

Note: The facilitator or designated recorder charts all ideas as they are stated.

Option: Collect the ideas using a round-robin approach. (Round-robin means that ideas are collected in an orderly fashion, by sequentially asking each person in the room for ideas.)

Option: Use two recorders to keep up with the fast flow of ideas.

Note: You may find a lull in ideas before a round of new and even more creative ideas. Don't be afraid of a few minutes of silence. If the group is stuck, take a break or read aloud all the ideas you have collected to that point.

3. When the group feels comfortable that there are no more ideas to add, go through the list of ideas, one by one. Ask the group if they need clarification or further information on what was meant by each item.

4. If necessary, narrow down the ideas to a few for further discussion and evaluation. Consider using MULTIVOTING, Technique 53, or NOMINAL PRIORITIZATION, Technique 57, as tools to help the group narrow down the number of ideas.

29

MINDMAPPING

Sometimes we brainstorm information and ideas that need to be subsequently placed into a specific sequence, order, or outline. But our group likes to brainstorm in a nonsequential manner, much like the process outlined in THE OLD-FASHIONED WAY. Is there an efficient way to brainstorm that will allow us later to sequence the information without extra work?

What is MINDMAPPING?

MINDMAPPING is a brainstorming technique for quickly charting your group's ideas in logical groupings, even when ideas are given in a nonsequential manner.

It is impossible to effectively outline ideas in a traditional, linear format while brainstorming. The MINDMAPPING technique allows you to efficiently brainstorm for ideas, and simultaneously create a skeletal framework for later categorization of the information you collect.

Examples of situations that benefit from MINDMAPPING include planning agendas or projects, identifying customer groups, or any other process that contains many components.

When do I use MINDMAPPING?

- When there will be many steps or issues to be remembered.
- When you are brainstorming information to be outlined or sequenced instead of brainstorming specific solutions to a problem.

  Note: MINDMAPPING works best when issues have many components and sub-components, or when there are a number of different categories of information provided. MINDMAPPING does not work well when brainstorming ideas will later be narrowed down to the best one or two ideas.

How do I use MINDMAPPING?

BEFORE THE MEETING

Identify specifically what you want to brainstorm. Plan an open-ended question to focus the brainstorming. You might say, for example:

SOURCE: Tony Buzan, *The Mind Map Book* (New York: Dutton, 1993).

92

What are the steps in completing this project? Which types of customers shall we target for testing our new product? What still needs to be done in order to finalize the annual report? What do we need to do to be prepared for the move to the new building next month?

Note: The first time you use MINDMAPPING with your meeting group, you will want to create two instructional charts. These charts should vividly illustrate how the MINDMAPPING process works and how it later translates into a linear format. Refer to Figs. 5-2 and 5-3 for examples of these charts.

DURING THE MEETING

1. Introduce the topic, the question, and the MINDMAPPING technique. For example:

As you know, our group is moving to the new building next year. I'd like your help in planning for that move. Let's start by MINDMAPPING your answers to the question, What do we need to do to be prepared for the move to the new building next year?

Note: If your group has never used MINDMAPPING before, take a few moments at this point to explain the process. You might say, for example,

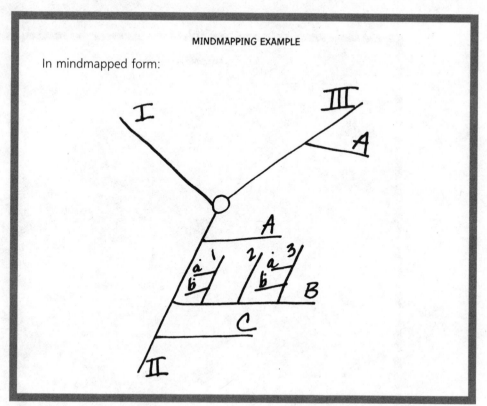

Figure 5-2. Example of MINDMAPPING.

We've never used the brainstorming technique called MINDMAP-PING *before. Basically it is a nonlinear way of outlining brainstormed information. This is an example of how it might look when it is finished* (refer to Fig. 5-2).

Basically, the main arms or branches that emanate from the circle at the center represent the primary ideas or categories that have been brainstormed. The secondary branches represent the subissues of the primary categories, the smaller branches are the subsets of the secondary categories, and so on. The idea is similar in structure to the old outline form that many of us learned in school, with Roman numerals, letters, and numbers. This chart (refer to Fig. 5-3) *is how the* MINDMAP (Fig. 5-2) *translates into this linear format. I will demonstrate as we go along.*

2. Prepare your own MINDMAPPING chart by drawing a circle in the middle of a clean sheet of chart paper. Write your topic or question (probably in abbreviated form) within the circle, or at the top of the chart.

   Option: Your chart could be created on an overhead.

MINDMAPPING EXAMPLE

In linear format:

I.

II.

    A.

    B.

        1.

           a.

           b.

        2.

        3.

           a.

           b.

    C.

III.

    A.

Figure 5-3. The same MINDMAPPING example in linear format.

3. Begin the brainstorming session, writing all your group's ideas down on the appropriate section of the MINDMAP. Brainstorm to an appropriate level of detail for your purpose. Continue to brainstorm until the group has exhausted all pertinent information or ideas.

   Option: If your MINDMAP is getting too complex and cumbersome, consider taking an arm of the MINDMAP and using it to create a new, separate, more specific MINDMAP.

   Figure 5-4 is an illustration of a completed MINDMAP, one that categorizes the information brainstormed for planning the summer company picnic.

4. After completing your mindmap, have the group sequence the information if appropriate. You might say, for example,

   Which of these arms or branches needs to be dealt with first? Which is next important?

   and so on. Number them as the group dictates and reproduce your outline in linear form if appropriate. Figure 5-5 is the resulting linear format outline created from the MINDMAP illustrated in Fig. 5-4.

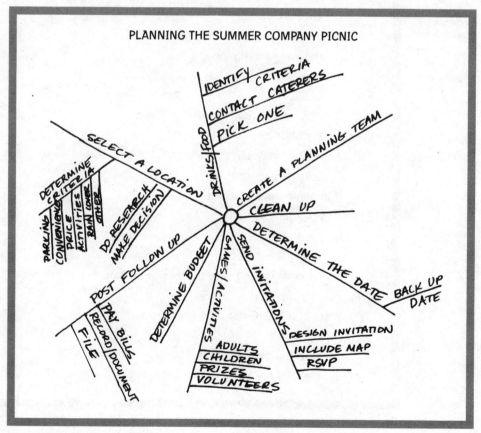

Figure 5-4. Completed MINDMAP for planning the summer company picnic.

PLANNING THE SUMMER COMPANY PICNIC IN LINEAR FORMAT

I.   Create a planning team
II. Determine the budget
III. Determine the date
   A. Select a backup date
IV. Select a location
   A. Determine criteria for preferred site
     1. Parking
     2. Convenience
     3. Price
     4. Rain cover
     5. Possibilities for activities
     6. Other
   B. Do research
   C. Make a decision
V.   Send invitations
   A. Design the invitation
     B. Include a map
     C. RSVPs
VI. Order food and drinks
   A. Establish criteria for caterers
   B. Contact possible caterers
   C. Select a caterer
VII. Plan games and activities
   A. For adults
   B. For children
   C. Determine prizes
   D. Determine need for volunteer coordinators
VIII. Plan for clean up
IX. Post-picnic follow-up
   A. Pay bills
   B. Record lessons learned
   C. Create a file for reference for next year

Figure 5-5. MINDMAP for planning the summer company picnic in linear format.

30

STORY BOARDING

Nonlinear brainstorming techniques seem to suit many of the groups I facilitate. Is there an alternative to MINDMAPPING that provides a flexible and visual process for sequencing information?

What is STORY BOARDING?

STORY BOARDING is a nonlinear brainstorming technique that allows you later to arrange the ideas your group generates into a desired order or linear format. Many brainstorming techniques are designed to seek specific solutions to a given question or problem. STORY BOARDING differs from these techniques because it provides a process to visually manipulate brainstormed information into the most desirable order or format.

Examples of specific items that benefit from STORY BOARDING include agendas, speeches, training programs, and any other project that requires the ability to move things around and look at information simultaneously.

When do I use STORY BOARDING?

- When you will want to categorize and sequence ideas at a later time.
- When you aren't sure how to structure things from the start.
- When brainstorming will identify only primary categories of information. (MINDMAPPING, Technique 29, is a better choice when subcategories need to be identified.)

How do I use STORY BOARDING?

BEFORE THE MEETING

After you select STORY BOARDING as the appropriate brainstorming technique, be sure that you <u>bring the necessary materials to the meeting.</u> These include markers or felt-tip pens, large cards (5″ × 8″ or larger) and tape, or large sticky notes.

Note: Because of their smaller size, sticky notes should only be used with small groups of fewer than five people.

If there is not an appropriate wall in the room to attach your cards, bring additional chart paper for this purpose.

Option: Bring a large bulletin board or foam board and straight pins, or any other surface that will allow you to attach and move cards around freely.

DURING THE MEETING

1. Introduce STORY BOARDING as a brainstorming technique that allows the group to categorize and sequence information at a later time.

2. As the group brainstorms, write each idea on a piece of paper or sticky note and post the notes randomly on a wall or other predetermined location.

3. When the brainstorming is finished, ask the group to help you sequence the items as appropriate based on the specific goal of the agenda item. See Fig. 5-6 as a finished example of STORY BOARDING, which uses the chapters of this book as its subject.

   Note: STORY BOARDING is similar to CARD CLUSTERS, Technique 31, in that both use cards or sticky notes to capture information. However, with STORY BOARDING, brainstorming is done as a group and information is later sequenced. With CARD CLUSTERS information is brainstormed individually and later categorized.

(1) Introduction: The Foundations	(2) Before the Meeting	(3) Improving Meeting Productivity	(4) Brainstorming Ideas
(5) Gathering Ideas	(6) Making Decisions	(7) Implementing Decisions	(8) Evaluating Meeting Effectiveness

Figure 5-6. Example of STORY BOARDING.

4. When the group agrees on a structure or an order, number each of the ideas in the determined sequence for documentation in the minutes.

   Note: It is a good idea to keep the STORY BOARD posted in a central location as a visual reminder of sequence. Make alterations if and when necessary.

31

CARD CLUSTERS

I know that sharing ideas is essential to our group's success. But ensuring that everyone's ideas are heard can be a slow and difficult process. Some people don't like to talk in front of a group, some people talk too much, and others continually judge ideas prematurely. I need a technique that is fast and efficient in gathering maximum input in minimum time. What do you suggest?

What is CARD CLUSTERS?

CARD CLUSTERS is a technique for gathering ideas and information quickly and efficiently, while eliminating common brainstorming problems.

The technique involves individually and silently writing ideas on cards, then categorizing the cards together as a group. The CARD CLUSTERS technique has been around for some time and is called different things by different professional groups. The technique is effective in any meeting where it is necessary to gather information quickly.

When do I use CARD CLUSTERS?

- When you want to get everyone's ideas but don't have much time.
- When some participants are not very verbal or like quiet time to think.
- When some participants tend to talk too much.
- When brainstormed information will need to be categorized.

How do I use CARD CLUSTERS?

BEFORE THE MEETING

1. <u>Identify the topic for discussion. Determine a specific OPEN-ENDED QUESTION</u> that will elicit the information you need (see Technique 34 for details). You might plan to ask, for example,

   What are the characteristics we desire in a new department manager?
   What issues do we need to address to decrease our turnaround time?
   What is our vision for the future of our company?

2. <u>Plan how you will use the gathered information.</u> Relative to the topics suggested above, you might plan to say, for example,

   This information will help us create a job description for the new department manager; or *We will use this information to determine which issues to address first;* or *This information will serve as the foundation for writing our group's vision statement.*

   Note: Information from CARD CLUSTERS can be used for many purposes. Other examples include: establishing goal areas or criteria categories, creat-

ing a shared understanding of a problem, and learning what participants need to know or already know.

3. Plan how you will introduce the topic at the meeting. Determine what background information to share.

4. Prepare the visual aids you will need to support the discussion. Charts or overheads of instructions are usually enough.

5. Acquire the necessary materials: sticky notes (or cards and masking tape) and
felt-tip pens for all participants.

   Note: Bring at least 30 sticky notes per person. Use felt-tip pens so that writ-
            ing can be seen from farther away.

6. Identify a space within the meeting room to place the sticky notes (or cards)
that the group will generate. You may choose a blank wall or put chart paper
or butcher paper over part of a wall.

   Note: Test the wall to be sure that the sticky notes will stick even if moved
            several times. Some sticky notes aren't very sticky at all! If you use cards
            and masking tape, a wall will work much better than chart paper.

IN THE MEETING

1. Introduce the agenda topic and your open-ended discussion question. Share
how the gathered information will be used. Use an instruction chart like the example illustrated in Fig. 5-7 to support your verbal instructions.

2. Ask everyone to brainstorm their ideas silently and individually about the specific question you asked. Ask them to write all their ideas on sticky notes, one
idea per sticky note.

   Note: Participate in the brainstorming unless you are a neutral facilitator.

3. Collect all written ideas and categorize them with other similar ideas.

   Option A: Ask everyone to bring their sticky notes up to the front of the room
             and place them on the wall or designated chart papers. Use a pre-
             pared chart similar to Fig. 5-8 to help you.

             Note: It's okay if there is more than one response that is the same.
             This shows any overlaps in thinking.

INDIVIDUAL EXERCISE

Please brainstorm your ideas to this question: (Your question here.)

- Write all your ideas on sticky notes.
- One idea per sticky note.
- Write in short phrases.
- Write as large as possible.

10 minutes—until 9:43

Figure 5-7. CARD CLUSTER guidelines.

WHEN YOU ARE FINISHED

- Put your sticky ideas up on the wall.
- Silently read others' sticky notes.
- Cluster your ideas with other similar ideas.

10 minutes—until 9:53

Figure 5-8. CARD CLUSTER instructions.

Option B: If there are more than 10 or 12 people in the meeting, it is impractical for everyone to participate in the clustering. Instead, ask a smaller group of volunteers to cluster the ideas. (Use the other participants' time wisely during this period. Have them work on something else or take a 10-minute break.) This smaller group can create headings for each category if they want, but it is not mandatory at this time. When the small group has finished, ask them to read aloud what they have put into each category. Gain agreement on what is in each category before moving on.

Option C: Ask each participant to choose one favorite idea and send it forward to you. Post all these ideas up on the wall. Read them aloud. Ask what ideas are similar to others. Begin to cluster ideas as appropriate. (Many ideas may not have clusters at this point.)

Next, ask participants to send up another favorite idea that is not already represented. With the group's help, cluster these new cards with other posted cards. Finally, ask participants to bring forward any other new ideas. Put each of them into the category that the group thinks is most appropriate.

4. Create headings for each cluster which summarize the common theme of all cards in that grouping. Headings should be short phrases, such as "Improved Communication" or "Mechanical Difficulties." Create heading cards for each cluster.

Option A: Have the group work together to create headings. Facilitate the discussion yourself or ask another participant to facilitate.

Option B: If the group is large, delegate categories to smaller subgroups. The easiest way to create smaller groups is to ask people sitting or standing next to each other to take one or two categories each. For example, *"Would the five of you please create a category name for this cluster of ideas?"* Give the subgroups a time limit of 5 to 10 minutes. After subgroups finish, ask them to share their heading ideas with the others for their approval.

Note: If your clusters are messy, draw lines around each cluster and its header cards, in order to make it easy to see what goes where.

5. Use the accumulated CARD CLUSTER information as planned.

101

32

STP

Often our discussions ramble from problem to solution and back again. Sometimes we even look for solutions before agreeing on what we want as an end result. What can we do to focus on one thing at a time without overstructuring ourselves?

What is STP?

STP (Situation, Target, Proposal) is a brainstorming technique designed to clarify a situation, define a target, and articulate a proposed solution. *Situation* refers to the current, undesirable state. *Target* refers to a future, desired state. The *Proposal* portion of the equation is the proposed plan of action to move from the current Situation to the desired Target.

Some people have the ability to jump from one category to another without problem or confusion. But this is not true for all individuals and it's certainly not true for groups of people. Focusing on one aspect of the process at a time avoids confusion and improves results.

When do I use STP?

- When an issue is multifaceted.
- When the group needs to determine where they are, where they want to be, and the best methods to get there.
- When you want to clarify issues for a presentation.
- When discussions seem to be unfocused and without direction.

How do I use STP?

1. Write Situation, Target, and Proposal on a white board or chart paper in three sections (refer to Fig. 5-9 as an example).
2. Brainstorming as a group, start with the first category on the chart, Situation. Ask the question: *"What do you see as the current situation?"*

   Note: Review the ground rules for your meeting and the guidelines for brainstorming, if necessary. See THE OLD-FASHIONED WAY, Technique 28, for brainstorming guidelines.

   Chart the group's responses.

SOURCE: Fred Fosmire, Sunriver, OR; DeltaPoint, Bellevue, WA.

Situation	Target	Proposal

Figure 5-9. Template example for STP.

Note: If ideas emerge from the discussion that belong in the Target or Proposal categories, chart them accordingly with permission from the person submitting the idea. If you find that the group is jumping all over the place, remind them to focus on the Situation category first.

3. After all ideas are charted, go back and <u>obtain agreement from the group on each of the brainstormed items.</u>

Note: It is important that the analysis of ideas follows the process of brainstorming. Do not analyze the ideas during the brainstorming portion of the process.

a. Read all of the brainstormed comments. Ask, *"Which comments need clarification?"*

b. Ask, *"Is there anything written here that you cannot agree with?"* Where disagreements exist, look for the cause of the disagreement and modify or clarify the statement as necessary.

Note: If there is a controversy or disagreement about any particular point and the conversation is bogging down, ask the group, *"How shall we handle this?"* You will want to find a balance between getting everything agreed upon and not getting bogged down. It may be a good idea to come back to a point of disagreement later, after the rest of the work in that section is complete.

Note: Be sure that the group is not stating the Situation as a Proposal. For example, the statement *"We don't have money for a new building"* presumes that a new building is a proposed solution to some problem. A better way to address the Situation would be to describe the current situation without bias as to the solution. For example, *"There are not enough desks, phones, and computers for everyone during peak periods of use."* Look at OPEN-ENDED QUESTIONS, Technique 34, as a technique to support you when this problem occurs. For example, you might ask, *"What specifically is causing you to conclude that we need a new building?"*

4. Once the Situation area is completed, <u>move to the next category, Target.</u> Target refers to defining your "preferred future," or the way the Situation would be if it were perfect or at least satisfactory. Ask the question, *"What would our situation be like if it were perfect?"*

   a. Brainstorm as before. Chart all responses.

   b. Seek consensus, modifying the ideas as necessary.

   Option: Before defining your Target, create a list of consequences that result from the current Situation. This reinforces why change is important.

5. <u>Use the same process for Proposal.</u>
   This may include brainstorming several solutions and picking one, or creating an action plan. See CHART ACTIONS, Technique 64, for details. Ask the question, *"How can we move from our current Situation to our preferred Target?"*

   a. Brainstorm as before. Chart all responses.

   b. Seek consensus, modifying the ideas as necessary.

6. <u>Use the resulting information</u> to start action, or to obtain approval to start action.

33

BREAKING A STALEMATE

Sometimes when we need to be the most creative, my participants seem to be restricted by their assumptions. I need to find a way to help them challenge those assumptions so we can generate a new level of thinking and creativity. What do you suggest?

What is BREAKING A STALEMATE?

BREAKING A STALEMATE is a brainstorming technique designed to challenge the paradigms and assumptions of your participants that seem to get in the way of their creative energy.

Instead of brainstorming solutions to a stated question or problem like other brainstorming techniques, BREAKING A STALEMATE brainstorms the assumptions upon which a given issue, product, or service is based, and then brainstorms creative alternatives that challenge or overturn these assumptions.

BREAKING A STALEMATE demands that your group look at doing business outside the accepted norms of that business.

When do I use BREAKING A STALEMATE?

- When your group is looking for a method to get ahead of the competition.
- When your group is stuck in old ways of doing business and you are afraid that this thinking will hamper the group's success in the future.

How do I use BREAKING A STALEMATE?

1. Introduce BREAKING A STALEMATE and why you are choosing to use the technique. You might say, for example:

As you know, our primary competition, X Corporation, is gaining on us fast. If we don't come up with a new way of doing business, we'll lose significant market share. And to make matters worse, X Corporation is owned by a multinational that traditionally throws money at marketing as a method to capture more market share. We can't win this battle fighting fire with fire, so let's look for a more ingenious and creative way to compete in the next decade.

SOURCE: Kenichi Ohmae, *Mind of the Strategist: The Art of Japanese Business* (New York: McGraw-Hill, 1982).

105

2. Have your participants <u>brainstorm an exhaustive list of all assumptions</u> that are accepted as common sense in their industry. For example: Petroleum is needed to run the engines in our factories. Insulation is the best way to save heat. Cars must travel on roads. Chart the group's responses.

3. <u>Brainstorm ways to overturn these assumptions.</u>

   Note: THE OLD-FASHIONED WAY of brainstorming will probably work best.

4. <u>Decide the best way to proceed,</u> usually in terms of research or other actions.

6

18 Techniques to Gather Information

Tameron's management team just spent the last hour reviewing the previous quarter's sales figures.

> *We can't afford to lose any more business. We've been pummelled in the marketplace over the past few years, and we just can't survive any more false starts. Why aren't we getting the same quality of information as other organizations seem to get?*

Organizations need to gather and analyze information in order to make intelligent decisions. This can be an arduous and daunting task. Because the quality of decisions inevitably suffers when based on incomplete and therefore inferior data, full information is absolutely essential. In today's world, this information comes both from inside and outside the organization, and often from nontraditional sources.

This chapter gives the meeting facilitator 18 techniques to accumulate maximum information in record time. Some of these techniques can be used to gather information before meetings, others are designed for use within meetings, and one technique, the DELPHI TECHNIQUE, is designed specifically for use in place of a meeting. The broad range of these techniques ensures that most every potential situation is covered.

Techniques are:

- 34 OPEN-ENDED QUESTIONS
- 35 INDIVIDUAL INTERVIEWS
- 36 FOCUS GROUPS
- 37 QUESTIONNAIRES
- 38 DELPHI TECHNIQUE
- 39 EXPECTATIONS SURVEY
- 40 PASSING NOTES
- 41 SKITS
- 42 IS/IS NOT

- 43 NOMINAL GROUP PROCESS
- 44 PROCESS FLOWCHARTING
- 45 CONTENT EXPERTS
- 46 PROUDS AND SORRIES
- 47 KEEP/THROW
- 48 WORKING BREAK
- 49 NEW SHOES
- 50 5 WHYS
- 51 SWOTS

34

OPEN-ENDED QUESTIONS

> What do you think?
>
> What ideas do you have?
>
> What are your reactions?
>
> Why is that?
>
> How can we do that?
>
> How do you like the plan?
>
> What alternatives would you suggest?

Sometimes when I ask a question, people just sit there and shrug their shoulders or blandly say yes or no. What can I do to stimulate more conversation?

What is OPEN-ENDED QUESTIONS?

OPEN-ENDED QUESTIONS is a technique for gathering information in a manner which invites the greatest response.

The way you form your questions determines the type of response you will receive. OPEN-ENDED QUESTIONS are questions that cannot be answered with a yes or no answer. *"What are your ideas?"* is an open-ended question. *"Do you have any ideas?"* is a closed-ended question because it can be answered with a simple yes or no response. Other examples of OPEN-ENDED QUESTIONS include: *"What ideas do you have?"* as opposed to *"Do you have any ideas?"* and *"What are your reactions to this plan?"* as opposed to *"Do you like this plan?"*

The use of OPEN-ENDED QUESTIONS presumes that participants have ideas or questions and that you are interested in hearing them. It is essential to use OPEN-ENDED QUESTIONS in order to ensure maximum participation.

When do I use OPEN-ENDED QUESTIONS?

- When you want to gather information.
- When you are interested in hearing the opinions of others.
- When your group tends to be silent.

How do I use OPEN-ENDED QUESTIONS?

BEFORE THE MEETING

1. As you plan for each agenda item, <u>determine specific open-ended questions that will elicit the type of information you need.</u> Decide how broad or narrow the focus of your question should be. For example: *"What is causing this increased error rate?"* or *"What is causing this increased error rate on the third shift production line?"* or *"What is causing this increased error rate on the third shift production line over the weekends?"*

   Note: Sometimes proposed solutions are disguised as OPEN-ENDED QUESTIONS. For example: *"How can we get the funding to hire another administrative assistant?"* is really a proposed solution. *"How can we resolve our paperwork backlog?"* would be a better question to solve the underlying problem.

2. Plan how you will share the purpose for the open-ended question. It is necessary to use a lead-in to the open-ended question, stating the purpose for the discussion. When a question is asked without knowing the purpose for the question, participants are often skeptical to respond. For example: *"We need to determine the best way to fix this problem. What have you heard about what's happening out on the shop floor?"*

Note: Most people ask closed-ended questions out of habit. To change your habits, consider tape recording your meeting or ask a participant to record the questions you ask throughout the meeting.

DURING THE MEETING

1. State the purpose for your question and ask your open-ended question/s. Consider posting the open-ended question/s on a chart or overhead.

Note: Be patient and wait for responses. And be careful. Meeting facilitators will often give some examples of "right answers," which can inadvertently turn their open-ended question into a closed-ended question. For example: *"What do you think is causing the increased error rate?"* (open-ended question); *"Is it the employees we hire?"* (closed-ended question).

Note: If you think you are getting responses that are too broad or too narrow, expand or contract your question.

2. Chart the responses.

Note: OPEN-ENDED QUESTIONS are a very important tool and should be used in virtually every technique when asking questions. See SHREDDED QUESTIONS, Technique 9, and 5 WHYS, Technique 50, as two specific examples.

Note: Closed-ended questions have their place. They are used to verify consensus or understanding of an issue. For example: *"Do we all agree?"* *"We're meeting next Thursday, right?"*

35

INDIVIDUAL INTERVIEWS

Sometimes we need to gather information from people other than those attending our meetings. On other occasions our limited meeting time needs to be spent making decisions instead of collecting information. Is there a technique you can suggest for these situations?

What is INDIVIDUAL INTERVIEWS?

INDIVIDUAL INTERVIEWS is a technique designed to gather information and ideas from specific stakeholders before a particular meeting takes place. Stakeholders are those people who have any vested interest, share, or stake in a given outcome. This information is generally collected and categorized for use in a specific meeting, but there are also times when INDIVIDUAL INTERVIEWS can take the place of a group meeting.

INDIVIDUAL INTERVIEWS ensures input, increases ownership, and helps guarantee that the processes used and the decisions made in your meetings will have the highest return on investment.

When do I use INDIVIDUAL INTERVIEWS?

- When information is needed from people other than those attending your meeting.
- When ideas and information can be gathered more efficiently on a one-to-one basis.
- When 100 percent meeting attendance is not possible.
- When the planned meeting time is too short for the quantity of information anticipated from the proposed agenda.
- When you want input from people about a decision that will ultimately be made by an individual or others not associated with the input group.

How do I use INDIVIDUAL INTERVIEWS?

1. As you plan your agenda, <u>determine what type of information or ideas must be gathered before the meeting, and how to best gather the information.</u> INDIVIDUAL INTERVIEWS are most often face-to-face, verbal exchanges.

   Option: Alternatives to INDIVIDUAL INTERVIEWS include telephone interviews, small group interviews (see FOCUS GROUPS, Technique 36), written questionnaires (see QUESTIONNAIRES, Technique 37), and E-mail interviews (see DELPHI TECHNIQUE, Technique 38).

2. Decide who should be interviewed.

  Note: Be sure to schedule interview times well before the actual meeting.

3. Plan the specific questions to ask during your interviews.

  Note: Refer to OPEN-ENDED QUESTIONS, Technique 34, and SHREDDED QUESTIONS, Technique 9, for support.

The type of information or ideas requested obviously will depend on the nature of your group, the meeting, and it's agenda.

- If you want to interview participants about their expectations for the meeting, you might ask, for example, *"What do you think are the most important issues for our group to address at our next meeting?"* or *"How do you think we are doing at working together as a group?"*

- If it is appropriate to interview employees about a specific process, product, service, or problem, you might ask, *"Where do you see the biggest opportunities for improvement?"* or *"How do you feel this specific problem should be addressed?"*

- If you want to question customers or suppliers about a specific issue, you might ask, *"What can we do to simplify our interactions with you?"* or *"Where do you see our best opportunities for improvement?"* or *"How do our products or services rate against our competitors'?"*

- If you choose to interview upper management about their perspective or considerations for your group planning session, you could ask, *"What information do we need from you before our planning discussions begin?"* or *"What do you expect specifically from our department in the next three years?"* or *"What do you think we are currently doing well?"* or *"Where do you see our biggest areas for improvement?"*

4. Determine who should ask the questions.

5. Decide how the information should be documented during the interviews.

  Option: Consider using a tape recorder during your interviews. This can avoid confusion about what was actually said when preparing documentation. Be sure to get permission from the interviewees beforehand.

  Note: If you use more than one person to conduct interviews, consider quality control measures to ensure consistency. Make sure there is congruity between interview questions and summarization techniques. Agree ahead of time on a system of documenting and compiling the information. It is possible for people to present oral reports, but these should be collaborated before the meeting for structural consistency. Let participants know if their comments will be on the record and credited to them.

6. Decide how the information and ideas collected will be summarized and presented at the meeting.

Note: Consider summarizing information into clustered categories, for example, by group or level within the organization. Determine which clustering method to use based on what you feel will reveal the best quality of information. Then determine if the information will be best presented with bullets or in narrative form.

Note: Be sure to get permission from interviewees if you quote them by name in the meeting.

7. Conduct your INDIVIDUAL INTERVIEWS.

8. Use the information as planned.

36

FOCUS GROUPS

We need to collect a lot of information from a large number of people in a short period of time. Face-to-face input is important, but our group doesn't have the time or the resources to gather this information through INDIVIDUAL INTERVIEWS. What do you suggest?

What is FOCUS GROUPS?

FOCUS GROUPS is a technique designed to gather information from groups of people. The need for this technique can be generated by time constraints, or the belief that the synergy of group discussions can create more input, ideas, concerns, and perceptions than one-on-one discussions.

FOCUS GROUPS are not recommended when you want quantitative or statistical types of information, but are excellent at providing qualitative information. FOCUS GROUPS can also be extremely effective when used in combination with INDIVIDUAL INTERVIEWS, Technique 35, and QUESTIONNAIRES, Technique 37.

FOCUS GROUPS are usually discussions with groups of eight to twelve people, and these groups generally contain a homogeneous selection of participants, e.g., a group of suppliers, customers, or employees from a specific department or level within an organization. Discussions usually last from one and a half to two hours and are facilitated by an interviewer or moderator. FOCUS GROUP data is collected to be used outside the FOCUS GROUP itself. The data provides information to the organization that can be used to improve its competitive position, its existing or future products or services, its work processes, or its organizational culture.

When do I use FOCUS GROUPS?

- When you want to gather information from a large number of people in a short amount of time.
- When you want to determine how specific decisions or actions are perceived within the organization.
- When you want to test the clarity of communication.
- When you want to generate hypotheses or new ideas.
- When you want to plan an organizationwide questionnaire.
- When you want to evaluate another group's ideas.
- When you are unfamiliar with opinions of specific groups and want to gain a broad idea quickly.

How do I use FOCUS GROUPS?

1. Clarify the information needed, why it is needed, and how it will be used.

Note: Agree that FOCUS GROUPS (or another technique) is the best process to gather the necessary information.

2. Determine who you will include in your FOCUS GROUPS. Examples include teams, levels or departments of employees, groups of suppliers or customers, groups of executives, managers or board members, community members, and special interest group members.

Note: Homogeneous groups where group members have something in common with each other work best.

Option: Consider using MINDMAPPING, Technique 29, to support you in identifying groups or specific participants within groups.

3. Determine the questions you will ask as well as the format of those questions.

Note: Use INTRODUCTIONS, Technique 1, as a technique to help participants become comfortable with each other. It is difficult for participants to be open without knowing who else is in the room. Food and beverages also give the meeting a more comfortable feel.

Review SHREDDED QUESTIONS, Technique 9, and OPEN-ENDED QUESTIONS, Technique 34, for ideas. Prepare an agenda for each FOCUS GROUP, an example of which can be found in Fig. 6-1.

SAMPLE AGENDA	
Introduction.	10 minutes
Review the purpose of meeting.	
Outline the structure of the meeting and how information will be used.	
Participant introductions.	
Questions.	75 minutes
What do you like best about our product/service?	
What do you like least about our product/service?	
What ideas for improvement do you have?	
Summary.	5 minutes
Plans for follow-up with participants.	
Thank you.	

Figure 6-1. Sample agenda for FOCUS GROUPS.

4. <u>Determine who will facilitate or moderate each focus group.</u> To ensure neutrality, consider using an external facilitator or a combination of internal and external persons.

5. <u>Determine how to document the information collected in the FOCUS GROUPS.</u> Chart responses, video or tape record responses, have a second person take notes during the meeting, or use a combination of these methods.

6. <u>Decide how information will be summarized.</u> Cluster in categories of information, categorize by focus group, or categorize by question asked.

7. <u>Prepare invitations for FOCUS GROUPS attendees,</u> including the following:
   - Purpose of the focus group
   - Who will be attending
   - Why and how participants were selected
   - Time and place
   - How long the meeting will last
   - Who will moderate or facilitate the focus group
   - Incentives for attendance (i.e., food, coffee, gifts, etc.)
   - Request for confirmation of attendance

8. <u>Prepare the logistics for the meeting.</u>

   Note: See Chap. 2 for ideas.

9. <u>Conduct the focus group.</u>

10. <u>Use the information as planned.</u>

    Note: In addition to entire books devoted to the subject of FOCUS GROUPS, there are a number of professional organizations that provide expertise in conducting FOCUS GROUPS. The information included here is designed to provide the fundamentals for facilitating FOCUS GROUPS.

37

QUESTIONNAIRES

I know that a number of organizations and facilitators use QUESTIONNAIRES to gather information. What can you tell me about them?

What is QUESTIONNAIRES?

QUESTIONNAIRES is a technique designed to gather information from individuals in writing. The information gathered can be quantitative, qualitative, or a combination of both. It is a relatively inexpensive technique that allows you to gather information from large numbers of people in a short period of time.

This technique does, however, have limitations. Because it is one-way communication, sometimes the data collected can be difficult to interpret. Some people will give you less information in writing than in person and you can receive lower response rates. But if utilized under the proper circumstances, QUESTIONNAIRES can be a valuable technique for gathering information.

There are five techniques described in this book that are designed to gather information outside actual meetings. QUESTIONNAIRES tends to be the least time-consuming of these techniques. The more time-consuming techniques, INDIVIDUAL INTERVIEWS, Technique 35, and FOCUS GROUPS, Technique 36, have already been described, and the DELPHI TECHNIQUE, Technique 38, and EXPECTATIONS SURVEY, Technique 39, will follow.

When do I use QUESTIONNAIRES?

- When you want to gather information from large groups of people.
- When gathering information in writing will meet the needs of your group.
- When you want to gather information from meeting participants before the meeting.

How do I use QUESTIONNAIRES?

1. <u>Determine the purpose and scope of the questionnaire</u> you are developing by asking yourself the following questions:
   - What is the purpose of your questionnaire?
   - Who is the audience for your questionnaire?
   - How will the information be used?
   - Who will use the results?
   - How will results be communicated?

2. <u>Develop your questionnaire,</u> choosing whether to structure your questions as open-ended or closed-ended in design. Following are three samples of how to design the same basic question. The first two are closed-ended examples and the last is open-ended. Note that questions can be expressed both as questions and as statements.

(A) My manager listens to my ideas.

Strongly Agree	( )
Agree	( )
Neither agree nor disagree	( )
Disagree	( )
Strongly Disagree	( )

(B) How frequently does your manager listen to your ideas?

Always	( )
Almost always	( )
Sometimes	( )
Rarely	( )
Never	( )

(C) Describe the way your manager listens to your ideas.

> *Note:* Effective closed-ended questions are very difficult to develop. Important responses can easily be omitted, and this can skew the validity of your questionnaire.

> *Note:* Open-ended questions gather a much wider breadth of information than closed-ended questions, but are much more difficult to summarize and statistically analyze. Choose the method that will work best for your purposes. You might also consider using both open- and closed-ended questions for different parts of your questionnaire.

When developing your questionnaire, consider the following basic guidelines:

- Be sure questions ask only one thing at a time.
- Use language that is easy to understand.
- Ask questions that are applicable to all who receive the QUESTIONNAIRE, or note exceptions clearly.
- Avoid asking leading or loaded questions, and questions where only partial alternatives are provided.
- Start with the least difficult and controversial questions.
- Cluster questions in relevant categories, unless you have a specific reason not to.

- Make the questionnaire look approachable. Crowded pages with small print are intimidating and give the impression that they will take a lot of time to complete.
- When you have the choice, shorter is better.
- With forced choice responses, be sure that there are equal numbers of positive and negative responses.
- Test your questionnaire for clarity and accuracy with a small sample of participants before sending it out to large groups of people. Consider using FOCUS GROUPS, Technique 36, to help plan the questionnaire.
- Include a cover letter clearly outlining the purpose of the questionnaire, who is receiving the QUESTIONNAIRE, a deadline for returning the questionnaire, and who to contact with problems or questions.

3. Determine the logistics of your questionnaire by answering the following questions:
   - Who will the questionnaires be returned to?
   - When do they have to be returned?
   - How will the questionnaires be distributed?
   - Who will write and who will sign the cover letter to accompany the questionnaire?
   - What publicity, if any, is appropriate?
   - How will the responses be compiled and by whom?
   - How will the results be summarized?
   - How, when, and by whom will the results of the questionnaire be communicated?

   Option: For large efforts, such as companywide surveys, or if you have little experience with QUESTIONNAIRES, consider hiring a professional firm to help you.

4. Administer the questionnaire.
5. Use the information as planned.

38

DELPHI TECHNIQUE

I need to gather information from a range of people in different locations. The information I require is relatively straightforward, but getting these people together is impossible. Help!

What is DELPHI TECHNIQUE?

The DELPHI TECHNIQUE is used to gather information and opinions from the members of a group without any face-to-face discussion. This occurs most often when it is logistically difficult for the group participants to get together. The process is carried out through a series of QUESTIONNAIRES, ending with a written summary given to each participant. Because the group using this technique will never meet, the entire process is executed through the mail, by fax, or by computer.

The DELPHI TECHNIQUE takes the place of a meeting, allowing participants the benefits of reviewing others' insights without physically interacting with them. However, sometimes the information gathered from this technique is used later in a meeting composed of a smaller or different group of people.

There are obvious limitations. The DELPHI TECHNIQUE requires much more time for the facilitator to prepare and, because there is no direct contact, it is difficult for participants to create a sense of team. Also, the success of the process depends significantly on the analytical and reporting skills of the facilitator.

When do I use DELPHI TECHNIQUE?

- When it is very difficult for participants to get together.
- When the focus is on one primary question or concern.
- When the contents of the discussion can easily be categorized and summarized for review.

How do I use DELPHI TECHNIQUE?

1. <u>Determine if the DELPHI TECHNIQUE is appropriate for your purpose.</u> If so, take the time to write a clear letter of introduction outlining the purpose and process you will use. Refer to 3P STATEMENTS, Technique 8, for support.

2. <u>Ask group members one or more questions as an initial inquiry that starts the process.</u> Questions should be open-ended questions such as, *"What are the problems in meeting holiday season customer demand?"* Be sure to explain the pur-

pose of the question and how the information will be used. Consider providing a questionnaire form that members complete and return by a specified date.

3. Tabulate the responses and include them on a second questionnaire that asks participants to vote for or rate the importance of various responses. See MULTIVOTING, Technique 53, or NOMINAL PRIORITIZATION, Technique 57, for ideas. In some cases, ask participants to write arguments or position papers justifying their reactions and reasoning.

4. Tabulate the ratings and summarize the arguments. Send the information back to group members and request that they reevaluate their selected choices. Continue this process until no new information is forthcoming and a consensus is reached.

5. Use the information as planned.

39

EXPECTATIONS SURVEY

Our group is planning where to focus our improvement efforts for the next few years. We want input from our customers and employees, but don't really know how to organize ourselves to get this input. What do you suggest?

What is EXPECTATIONS SURVEY?

EXPECTATIONS SURVEY is a technique designed to gather quantifiable information from customers of a specific group. In this case, a group can mean a company, division, department, or team within any organization. An EXPECTATIONS SURVEY measures the expectations of a group from a wide variety of customers. This information then provides a basis for examining priorities and setting goals.

The term customer not only refers to the traditional concept of the customer, who is typically the end user or purchaser of an organization's products or services. Today, a customer is defined as anyone who is impacted by a group's products or services. This includes the traditional customer noted above, as well as employees, management, stockholders, suppliers, lenders, and others. These customers have roots both inside and outside an organization.

Without input from its customers, no group can ever have a complete picture of its top priorities. Understanding the needs and priorities of customers has become trendy because it makes good business sense. Any group or organization that neglects to do so will be likely to experience rework, loss of market share, and unnecessary conflict over priorities.

When do I use EXPECTATIONS SURVEY?

- When preparing to plan group or team goals.
- When you want to establish priorities for improvement.
- When you want feedback from your customers.

How do I use EXPECTATIONS SURVEY?

1. <u>Present the purpose of the EXPECTATIONS SURVEY</u> to your meeting group. For example:

   EXPECTATIONS SURVEY is a technique for gathering information and feedback from all the customers of a group, both inside and outside the organization. This information measures the perceived expectations of these customers and provides a basis for decision making and goal setting.

   To support your efforts, you might ask the group,

SOURCE: Caryn Spain, Applied Business Solutions, Seattle, WA.

What would you see as the advantage of our asking customers for their expectations? What would be the disadvantages? How could we use this information to help us plan our improvement efforts?

2. <u>Determine which customer groups to ask for feedback.</u> Be sure to include all customers that are impacted by the activities of your specific meeting group. Consider MINDMAPPING, Technique 29, as a tool for brainstorming and categorizing information.

3. <u>Make logistical decisions.</u> You might ask the group, for example,

   Will the survey be executed in person or in writing? Who will conduct and coordinate gathering the responses? What are the time frames involved?

4. <u>Agree how to prepare the information for analysis at your next meeting.</u> Determine the specifics by asking, *"Who will do what, by when?"*

5. <u>Agree on an appropriate amount of time to follow up with your customers.</u> This follow-up will test your group's progress toward the improvements identified by your customers.

6. <u>Plan how to communicate to your customers about the EXPECTATIONS SURVEY.</u> Agree on any written communication to each customer group. Be sure to clearly communicate the purpose of the survey when communicating with your customers. For example:

   We are currently planning how to serve you better in the future. Please help us to plan appropriately by sharing your expectations of our group, how important each of these expectations is to you, and how well we are currently meeting those expectations.

7. <u>Prepare EXPECTATIONS SURVEY sheets,</u> an example of which is shown in Fig. 6-2.

8. <u>Conduct the EXPECTATIONS SURVEY.</u>

   Note: Be sure to coach any interviewers to remain neutral and nondefensive. Issues will surface that might surprise the interviewers, and their reactions may impact the quality of the response. Remind them that all feedback is valuable feedback, even if it exposes a misunderstanding between the customer and the group. While on-the-spot problem solving of little problems is sometimes acceptable, the goal of the EXPECTATIONS SURVEY meeting is information gathering, not problem solving.

9. <u>Collect and tabulate all the information.</u> Cluster information together as is appropriate and possible. It may be helpful to sort the information by different types of customer.

   Note: Look for the biggest gaps, where the level of importance is very high and the level of current satisfaction is very low. These are the areas where you have the largest opportunities for improvement and where your clients will take notice. Figure 6-3 provides an illustration.

   As you can see from the example, providing accurate reports and giving advance warning about upcoming changes are the most important opportunities for improvement in this EXPECTATIONS SURVEY.

Customer Expectations	Level of Importance 1 Low 5 High	Level of Current Satisfaction 1 Low 5 High
List your expectations of our group. Please be as specific as possible.		

Figure 6-2. Sample template for EXPECTATIONS SURVEY.

10. Use this information in planning goals for the next period. This period could be six months, one year, two years, or whatever period is practical given the nature of the information collected. (See SMART GOALS, Technique 63, for support.)

11. Communicate to your customers involved in the EXPECTATIONS SURVEY what you found and what your group intends to do with the information. Share the specific goals you have set in response to the information.

12. After the agreed upon time frame, return to your customers for additional feedback. Ask them once again for their expectations of your group, their ranking of these expectations, and their current level of satisfaction. Benchmark the progress of your efforts after one year.

   Note: This is a process that your group could continue or modify on an annual or otherwise regular basis.

Customer Expectations	Level of Importance 1 Low 5 High	Level of Current Satisfaction 1 Low 5 High
List your expectations of our group. Please be as specific as possible.		
Return phone calls within half a day.	4	4
Provide accurate reports.	5	2
Give us advance warning about changes that will affect the way we work.	5	1
Communicate to our support staff in a professional manner.	4	3

Figure 6-3. Sample of completed EXPECTATIONS SURVEY.

40

PASSING NOTES

Several of the groups within our organization are interdependent. Productivity suffers because none of the groups seems to understand exactly how their own work impacts the other groups. And the atmosphere that has developed is more competitive than collaborative. We want to find an effective way to give each other feedback, but we need to learn a technique that is not heavy-handed. Do you have any ideas?

What is PASSING NOTES?

PASSING NOTES is a technique for giving and receiving specific feedback to and from other divisions, departments, groups, work shifts, or even individuals within an organization. The purpose and goal of PASSING NOTES are very serious but the process is achieved in a lighthearted manner.

The ultimate objective of the PASSING NOTES exercise is to help specific, interdependent groups or individuals understand what other groups or people need from them in order to do their jobs more effectively. The beauty of PASSING NOTES is that everybody learns and everybody wins.

When do I use PASSING NOTES?

- When you have groups or individuals that are dependent on each other but have not communicated very well in the past.
- When you want to set up a goal-setting session by sharing feedback and information first.
- When you want to help groups, or individuals within a group, understand their interdependence and what the others need to work more effectively with them.

How do I use PASSING NOTES?

BEFORE THE MEETING

1. Plan how you will use PASSING NOTES in the meeting.

 Note: This exercise is generally done in a large group session with smaller work group breakouts. It can also be done among individuals within a group.

 Note: You will need to allot approximately 90 minutes for this exercise.

2. Create the instructional charts or overheads you will use (see Figs. 6-4 through 6-7 for examples).

DURING THE MEETING

1. Present the purpose of PASSING NOTES. You might say, for example:

We are a group of people who are dependent upon each other for success. But we haven't taken much time to communicate what we need from each other to be successful. We will take the next hour and a half to exchange information, and then use that information to make plans to help support each other's efforts better.

2. Break participants into their specific work groups. Ask each group to write PASS-ING NOTES to all of the groups they are dependent upon to get their own work done. These PASSING NOTES should address a specific statement, question, or issue. This might be introduced as, for example,

In order for us to meet our goals, we need you to ... or In order for us to work more effectively, we need you to ...

Display the PASSING NOTES guidelines chart or overhead you prepared before the meeting, an example of which is illustrated in Fig. 6-4.

PASSING NOTES

Answer this question for each of the other groups you work with: *"In order for us to meet our goals (or work more effectively) with you, we wish you would ..."*
    Be sure to:

- Honor the self-esteem of others.
- State the rationale for your request.
- Make your request in concrete, specific, and measurable terms.

20 minutes

Figure 6-4. Guidelines for PASSING NOTES chart.

Coach your groups on how to give constructive feedback, and offer specific guidelines for how to respond to PASSING NOTES in positive terms. All feedback must honor the self-esteem of others, state the purpose of the request, and make the request in concrete, specific, and measurable terms. For example, one note might read:

We need more lead time in order to get you the materials you need when you want them. We would appreciate your communicating with us as soon as you hear from your customers with even an estimate of your needs. When everything is crystallized from your end we can finalize the order, but we would appreciate the opportunity to plan ahead better.

Note: Unless you are a neutral facilitator, participate with your group.

3. When finished, ask each group or individual to distribute their PASSING NOTES.

4. Ask each group to read all their PASSING NOTES. They are allowed to ask for clarification but rebuttals or excuses are not allowed. Post the instructional chart or overhead you have prepared for this section, similar to Fig. 6-5.

READ YOUR NOTES

- Read all your notes. Formulate any questions for clarification. (10 min.)
- If needed, send representatives to different groups to get clarification. No rebuttals or excuses are permitted. Just listen. Representatives take notes and summarize what they heard before returning to their own group. (10 min.)
- Representatives report what they learned. (10 min.)

30 minutes total

Figure 6-5. Instructions chart for PASSING NOTES.

5. When finished, ask each group to start problem solving the issues expressed in their PASSING NOTES. This will result in a list of corrective action items that they can commit to. (See THE OLD-FASHIONED WAY, Technique 28, for details.) Post a chart or overhead similar to Fig. 6-6 to support your instructions.

GROUP COMMITMENTS

- Pick a recorder, a reporter, and a timekeeper.
- Respond to each NOTE, one at a time. Brainstorm as necessary.
- Agree on corrective actions, document on charts. Include a contact or coordinator name for each action.

20 minutes

Figure 6-6. Problem-solving chart for PASSING NOTES.

6. Next, ask each group to report their action plans for all the PASSING NOTES they received. The group sending each NOTE then responds to the action plans with a thumbs-up (affirm) or thumbs-down (deny) signal. Coach the groups giving thumbs-down signals to briefly explain why they don't accept the action plan. Plan about 10 minutes for every group reporting back. Post an instructional chart similar to Fig. 6-7 during this section.

Option: If you have more than three or four groups, or if your PASSING NOTES came from individuals instead of groups, consider having representatives go back to each group to get one-on-one feedback instead of having a group report back.

7. If necessary, ask groups to plan another meeting to work on issues left unresolved between themselves and other groups. If possible, have this "unresolved issues" meeting immediately after Step 8. Dismiss all groups who have no un-

> **PASSING NOTES ACTION REPORTS**
>
> - Report your action plans for each note received.
> - Pause to get a Thumbs-Up or Thumbs-Down reply from the sender group. Any Thumbs-Down is noted on a chart paper for later discussion.
>
> 10 minutes per group

Figure 6-7. Action plan instructional chart for PASSING NOTES.

resolved issues and ask those remaining to make necessary changes to get a thumbs-up approval.

Note: The "unresolved issues" meeting would follow the steps outlined in 4, 5, and 6 above.

8. <u>Plan a follow up session or progress report,</u> including a specific date and time whenever possible.

41

SKITS

We are constantly trying to maximize the efforts of our organization. But it's difficult to know how to help work teams without knowing exactly what they do or the problems they face. How can I lead work groups to share this kind of information without being boring?

What is SKITS?

SKITS is a technique for groups to share information about their responsibilities and work situation with other groups in their organization. In this way they can help others better understand the reality of their situation.

SKITS uses the power of example to illustrate a position, depict a problem, or illuminate a typical work situation. In addition to being a fun and creative group exercise, SKITS can be an extremely effective technique that exposes emotional, difficult, and frustrating work situations in memorable, profound, and powerful ways.

When do I use SKITS?

- When it is important to share job information with other departments.
- When you want to illustrate a feeling or point that is not easily explained in words alone.
- When you want to get a point across in an interesting, memorable way.

How do I use SKITS?

1. <u>Ask participants from each group represented in the meeting to create a SKIT that describes what it is like to work in their department.</u> Include as much information as possible, such as the atmosphere, roles, responsibilities, and frustrations they might feel.

   a. Have each group first agree on the key points they would like to make in their SKIT.

   b. Next ask them to plan the best way to portray those points in their SKIT.

   This information is best presented on a chart, as in Fig. 6-8.

   In addition, establish clear ground rules for the exercise by posting a chart as illustrated in Fig. 6-9.

   c. Allow approximately 15 to 30 minutes for preparation.

Figure 6-8. Instructional chart for SKITS.

Note: To begin, it is a good idea to allow 15 to 20 minutes for preparation. About 13 minutes into the exercise, ask each group how they are doing and allow them to negotiate for more time if necessary.

Option: Groups could come to the meeting already prepared to present their SKITS.

2. Have the groups present their SKITS.

3. Debrief the SKITS.
The debriefing exercise should take place in small work groups. Use the same debrief questions for each SKIT, as shown in Fig. 6-10. The group who presented the SKIT does not debrief its own SKIT.

4. Have each group report back with a summary of their discussions.

Note: If you have more than one group debriefing the same SKIT, have each of those groups share their debriefing of that same SKIT before moving on to debrief other SKITS.

Figure 6-9. Ground rules chart for SKITS.

SKITS DEBRIEF QUESTIONS

- What were the key points you observed?
- What points need clarification?
- What was your reaction?
- What can your department or you do to diminish the frustrations you observed in this skit?

15 minutes debrief for each SKIT presented

Figure 6-10. Debriefing chart for SKITS.

5. Ask each group to create an action plan based on the information contained in their summaries. You might introduce this section by asking, for example, *"What can your department or you do to improve communication and diminish the frustrations you observed in this skit?"* Allow 20 minutes for this section. Each action plan should be typed and distributed as soon as possible after the meeting.

6. Ask the group to define when and how it is best to follow up. Take responsibility to make sure that the follow-up does occur in the manner and time frame that the group agrees to.

42

IS/IS NOT

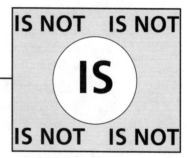

We have a demanding problem to solve and we're finding it difficult to get our arms around it. Is there a simple technique that will focus our efforts in the right direction?

What is IS/IS NOT?

IS/IS NOT is a technique for specifically identifying a problem. *"A problem well stated is a problem half solved."* As the old adage reveals, a problem can't be solved until it is clearly and accurately identified. IS/IS NOT defines exactly what a problem is and what a problem is not.

Sometimes the process of isolating a problem is quite simple. *"The problem is not that the order is a week late. The problem is that you didn't communicate with us."* At other times, a problem is so ambiguous or complex that it demands a lengthy process of questioning and analysis. For example, *"What is causing our company to lose money?"* may be too complicated a question to correctly diagnose with only IS/IS NOT. But this technique will appropriately steer participants to further in-depth analysis.

The IS/IS NOT technique surrounds a problem like a net surrounds a school of fish. As the net is drawn in a little bit at a time, tighter and tighter, some fish escape because they are unwanted while others are trapped and can't find their way out. Once the net is finally pulled in, the true nature and size of the catch are revealed. The fishermen then analyze their catch, throwing out what is not useful to keep, and keeping only that which will benefit them.

When do I use IS/IS NOT?

- When your group is not sure about the cause of a problem.
- When a problem needs to be isolated.
- When the true nature of a conflict between groups or individuals is not clear.

How do I use IS/IS NOT?

1. <u>Explain IS/IS NOT and how your group will use it</u> to define the nature of the problem you are addressing. For example:

SOURCE: Charles H. Kepner and Benjamin B. Tragoe, *The Rational Manager* (New York: McGraw-Hill, 1965).

IS/IS NOT is a technique for helping us isolate the problem we face. By asking a series of questions about what the problem is and what the problem is not, we will be able to clearly articulate our problem. Then we can work on how to solve the problem.

2. <u>Ask your meeting group a series of questions pertinent to their own situation.</u>

   a. You might ask, for example, *"Where does the problem happen?" "When does the problem happen?" "How does it happen?" "What processes and people are involved?"*

   b. And then you might ask, *"Where else could the problem occur, but it doesn't?" "When could the problem occur, but it doesn't?" "Where are the same people, processes, and materials being used but without this problem?"*

      Option: Make two columns on a chart or overhead, one for what you know the problem IS, one for what you know the problem IS NOT. Record the group's answers appropriately.

   Note: Depending on the nature of the problem, groups may need to go out to find information and discuss their findings at a later meeting.

3. <u>Review</u> your IS/IS NOT <u>data.</u>

4. <u>Agree on the focus of the problem.</u>

5. <u>Plan to test the cause</u> of the problem as necessary.

6. <u>Plan how to address and solve</u> the problem.

43

NOMINAL GROUP PROCESS

Our group needs some discipline. A few outspoken people seem to be influencing the thinking of the other meeting participants. If we are to truly benefit from everyone's ideas, we need to find a way to eliminate this type of pressure. Do you have any ideas?

What is NOMINAL GROUP PROCESS?

NOMINAL GROUP PROCESS is a technique that allows meeting participants to express themselves without immediate outside influence. The process involves having each group member individually write down his or her thoughts about an issue or problem before presenting them to the group verbally.

NOMINAL GROUP PROCESS provides the time for participants to collect and articulate their own thoughts before they hear other perspectives. This creates fuller participation, and assures that the valuable input of the whole is not impacted and altered by the most persuasive individuals in the group.

When do I use NOMINAL GROUP PROCESS?

- When you want to make sure individuals are doing their own thinking.
- When you want to be sure that you hear from everyone in the meeting group.
- When you need a method to collect maximum ideas in minimal time.

How do I use NOMINAL GROUP PROCESS?

1. Introduce the issue or problem under consideration and the NOMINAL GROUP PROCESS technique. You might say, for example,

   Before we can solve this problem, we need to understand it clearly. Each of you has a slightly different perspective on the problem because of your different experiences and areas of expertise. To help us to fully understand everyone's point of view, let's use a technique called NOMINAL GROUP PROCESS. This technique will allow us each to spend a few minutes thinking quietly and individually about the problem. We will then share

SOURCE: A.L. Debecq and A.H. Van de Ven, "A Group Process Model for Problem Identification and Program Planning," *Journal of Applied Behavioral Science, 7,* 1971.

our perspectives with each other so that we will have a more complete picture to consider.

2. <u>Ask all members to write down their ideas about the specific problem under consideration.</u> Present the issue as a specific question or set of open-ended questions (see OPEN-ENDED QUESTIONS, Technique 34), and post your questions on chart paper or an overhead. For example:

    We're having a problem delivering our goods on time. When does it happen? What is happening? Who is it happening to? What is the cause of the problem?

    Option: Meeting participants can be asked to come to the meeting already prepared to share this information.

3. <u>Ask participants to share their thoughts, facts, or ideas with the group</u> one at a time.

    a. Chart each person's comments, one chart for each question asked.

    Note: Post all charts around the room when the pages are full. (The participants will need them as visual aids later on.)

    b. Allow other participants to ask questions for clarification, but not to evaluate or elaborate further at this time.

    Option: Hold off on all questions for clarification until after all ideas from all participants have been documented.

4. <u>Review all the information in subgroups or as a whole.</u>

    Option A: Make a summary list that includes all information while eliminating duplications.

    Option B: Review all information and select the three or four ideas that are most worthy of further exploration. Consider using MULTIVOTING, Technique 53.

    Option C: Ask the group: *"What patterns do you see? In what areas do we have general agreement? In what areas are there significant disagreements? What conclusions can we draw from this information? What additional information do we need to gather?"* Chart the group's responses.

5. <u>As a group, define the problem with one statement that deals comprehensively with all the information gathered.</u> Use that statement as a basis for problem solving.

    Option: If, because of your group's specific situation, it is inappropriate to create a statement for problem solving, decide as a group how to proceed.

44

PROCESS FLOWCHARTING

We want to make improvements to our processes but we don't know where to begin. How can we gather information about what is happening with a process that goes through many hands and even many departments?

What is PROCESS FLOWCHARTING?

PROCESS FLOWCHARTING is a technique for identifying, documenting, and analyzing all the steps in an existing process, and then looking for methods to improve that process. "Process" in this situation is defined as any series of progressive and interdependent steps to achieve some end result.

People very often are not cognizant of all the steps involved in a process. Because of this lack of awareness, people can be very critical and intolerant of the concerns and perspectives of others. When there is an understanding of specifically how a current process works, it is easier to look for opportunities to improve and streamline it.

PROCESS FLOWCHARTING can be an eye-opener for groups who are unaware of all that must be done to accomplish a specific task, and thus serves as an effective approach to analyzing and improving existing processes.

When do I use PROCESS FLOWCHARTING?

- When you need to analyze a process or problem that involves many steps and many people.
- When people disagree on what is happening, what should happen, or why things need to happen.
- When you need to save time, money, or resources by improving efficiency.
- When parts of a process are causing problems but you cannot easily identify the best methods for fixing the problem.
- When creating a job aid or formalizing a procedure.

How do I use PROCESS FLOWCHARTING?

BEFORE THE MEETING

1. Determine what process will be analyzed.
2. Determine where in the process to begin your analysis, where to finish and at what level of detail. You might plan to say, for example,
   We will examine the bill payment process from the time an invoice is received in our office until the time that it is paid. We will look at the process in sufficient detail that we can all understand how much time is needed for each specific step.
3. Determine who needs to be involved. Be sure to include all people who are involved in the process.

Note: With very large processes, include representatives of all groups involved.

4. <u>Assemble necessary materials:</u> enough sticky notes, felt-tip pens, and chart paper for the meeting.

DURING THE MEETING

1. <u>Explain the purpose of PROCESS FLOWCHARTING.</u> You might <u>introduce the topic</u> by saying, for example,

PROCESS FLOWCHARTING is a technique for identifying all the steps in an existing process and looking for ways to improve that process.

2. <u>As a group, list the steps</u> involved between the beginning and the end of the process.

Note: Look to those who actually perform any specific step to give you the information on what is involved in that step.

Use a sticky note for each step in the process (so that you can move things around if you have forgotten anything). Place each sticky note on your chart paper, one after another.

Note: Most processes involve many steps and will require three to four sheets of chart paper taped together. You might want to consider using large sheets of butcher paper instead.

Note: If you encounter a portion of the process that no one in the room is familiar with, make a note of it and keep moving forward.

When the process comes to a decision point, split your flowchart in as many directions as options become available at the decision point. Follow each new direction when appropriate, or make a note to see another flowchart for details when this happens. A decision point is revealed by a closed-ended question, one that can only be answered either yes or no. If yes, one activity happens, if no, another activity happens. You might express this situation as follows:

Is the form completed correctly? If the form has all the information on it, the order is filled. If the form doesn't have all the necessary information, it is put in a box labeled "incomplete."

Note: These decision points can expose significant amounts of waste and unnecessary work.

3. When finished with the PROCESS FLOWCHART, <u>review the completed chart for possible gaps or inconsistencies.</u> Plan to show the chart to others familiar with the process to help you identify any missing areas, increase understanding of current processes, and verify the accuracy of the chart.

4. If necessary, <u>assign symbols and redraw the resulting chart.</u> A sample of potential symbols is illustrated in Fig. 6-11.

5. With the group, <u>analyze the current process</u> illustrated on the PROCESS FLOWCHART. Figure 6-12 illustrates an example of what an invoicing PROCESS FLOWCHART might look like.

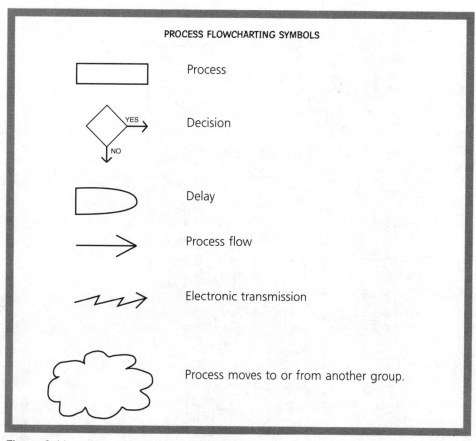

Figure 6-11. Sample symbols for PROCESS FLOWCHARTING.

Identify problems, unnecessary steps, and methods for measuring improvement. With help from all involved, look for waste, rework, and non-value-added steps.

6. <u>Brainstorm and agree on changes to improve the process.</u> Create a new PROCESS FLOWCHART as a tool for documenting these changes.

   Note: Consider documenting the expected anticipated time and cost savings from these changes.

7. <u>Test the new process.</u> Plan how to communicate the changes to others involved in the process, and establish a specific follow-up time to measure how well the changes are working.

8. <u>Meet again at a predesignated time to review how well the changes are working.</u> Make modifications at that time and look for additional ways to make the process more effective.

   Note: For very complex processes, consider utilizing available computer software to support your analysis.

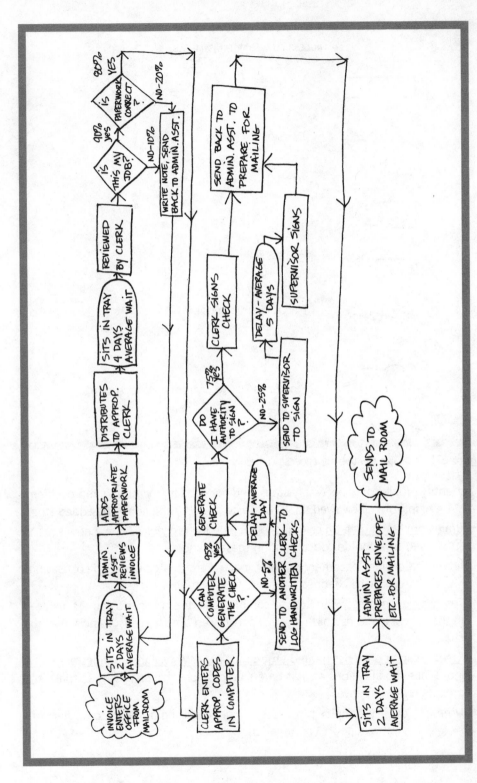

Figure 6-12. Sample of an invoicing PROCESS FLOWCHART.

45

CONTENT EXPERTS

Sometimes our group needs to hear from experts in various fields in order to understand more about a technical issue. But whenever we have an expert come in to talk, things never go as planned. They either talk over our heads, talk too long, or totally miss the point we are seeking. How can I work more effectively with these people?

What is CONTENT EXPERTS?

CONTENT EXPERTS is a technique for gathering information on a specific subject from someone who does it for a living, studies it for a living, or uses it for a living. These people can come both from inside and outside the organization, and they may be persons several levels above or below you in the organization.

CONTENT EXPERTS can only be successful when they clearly understand the purpose for talking to your group, the current level of understanding of the group, and the parameters of the discussion. These parameters can include time, the amount of two-way communication expected, and any anticipated questions.

It is the responsibility of the meeting facilitator to strictly control these CONTENT EXPERTS in order to provide the meeting group with a relevant, clear message and a helpful basis upon which to move forward.

When do I use CONTENT EXPERTS?

- When you need to get information or an opinion based on expert knowledge.
- When a controversial issue is best addressed by an outsider.
- When the group is interested in learning new skills or perspectives.

How do I use CONTENT EXPERTS?

BEFORE THE MEETING

1. After defining the purpose of this part of your meeting, <u>brainstorm the best methods to gather information.</u> You might ask yourself, for example:

   Who would know the answers to our questions? Who could we invite to our next meeting to shed some light in this issue for us? Is having a person come to speak to us the best way for us to gather the information we need?

Option: Consider films, articles, panel discussions, and field trips as possible alternatives.

If you choose to use CONTENT EXPERTS, question people within your organization, colleagues, or professional organizations to find out who is the best person for your purposes.

Note: Be sure not to overlook the CONTENT EXPERTS working within your organization. For example, the best people to discuss a certain type of machinery are the crew that uses that machinery. And don't forget to tap a person from a competitor company who has recently joined your firm.

2. <u>When you contact the CONTENT EXPERTS whose services you desire, clearly state the purpose of your request.</u> If they agree to participate, tell them how to best prepare for your meeting. For example, you might want to share answers to the following questions:

- Who are the audience?
- What does the audience want to know?
- What level of current knowledge do the meeting participants have?
- What level of detail would the group like the expert to provide?
- What type of presentation do participants expect?
  (Will the presentation be formal or informal? Will questions and answers be encouraged during the presentation or held to the end?)
- How much time will the expert have to speak?
  (Tell the CONTENT EXPERTS that your group is committed to staying within time frames and that you will use a timekeeper to help you keep on track.)
- What visual aids will be available for use?
- What compensation can the group provide?

  Note: External experts will likely expect to be compensated for their time. Letters of recognition to supervisors are appropriate for internal experts, and sometimes this is even adequate for external people.

3. <u>Follow up your conversation with written confirmation.</u> Follow up again the day before the meeting to confirm all the details.

4. <u>Schedule the CONTENT EXPERTS at the beginning of the meeting,</u> so that if your agenda slides, you do not keep them waiting.

DURING THE MEETING

1. <u>Introduce your guest.</u> Give your group some guidelines for the presentation. Negotiate these guidelines with both the CONTENT EXPERTS and your group. Ask for a timekeeper, or act as the timekeeper yourself.

2. <u>Listen to the presentation.</u>

DEBRIEFING QUESTIONS

1. Choose a recorder or reporter and timekeeper
2. Answer these questions:
   - What conclusions can we draw from listening to this expert?
   - What actions should we consider?
   - What recommendations do we have as a group?

15 minutes

Figure 6-13. Debriefing chart for CONTENT EXPERTS.

3. After the presentation, take at least a few minutes to <u>debrief and plan appropriate follow-up.</u> Depending on the size of your group, consider either a large group discussion, or small group discussions. See SMALL GROUPS, Technique 20, for details. Post the debriefing questions (see the sample in Fig. 6-13).

   Note: You may want to ask the content expert to stay during this discussion to answer any remaining questions or concerns.

4. Based on the answers to the debriefing questions, <u>make decisions for action or follow-up as is appropriate</u> for your group.

AFTER THE MEETING

1. <u>Send a thank-you note to your guest.</u> Include a copy to the person's supervisor if suitable.
2. When appropriate, pay the content expert in a timely manner. <u>Follow up on any other commitments made</u> as soon as possible.

46

PROUDS AND SORRIES

Our group has been through a lot together and we've developed some serious emotional energy about how we worked with each other in the past. It's difficult to articulate exactly what all the issues are, but I want to use this energy and past experience to help us in the future. What do you suggest?

What is PROUDS AND SORRIES?

PROUDS AND SORRIES is a technique designed to constructively address both the positive and potentially negative emotional issues facing your meeting group. Because emotional issues can impact heavily on the effectiveness of any group, it is imperative for you to have a technique in your arsenal to deal effectively with these types of problems. Overlooking these emotional issues or pretending that they don't exist can be disastrous.

PROUDS AND SORRIES helps a group come to terms with its past. The technique analyzes, in a methodical way, what the group's participants feel proud about and what they feel sorry about. This information is used to clear the air, and as a springboard for discussions to establish norms, goals, and objectives for the future.

Emotional energy is common within work groups. It is especially strong in organizations that are downsizing and going through dramatic change, in groups where a project has ended negatively, and in organizations that have been purchased or taken over by another group. PROUDS AND SORRIES allows people to own up and move on.

When do I use PROUDS AND SORRIES?

- When there are many hard feelings among group members.
- When you want to allow people to share feelings about a project in a constructive, focused manner.
- When you want to use the past to build on the future.

How do I use PROUDS AND SORRIES?

BEFORE THE MEETING

1. <u>Assemble necessary materials:</u> enough sticky notes, marking pens, and chart paper to bring to the meeting.
2. <u>Create the charts you will use</u> (see Figs. 6-14 through 6-16).

SOURCE: Marvin Weisbord, *Discovering Common Ground* (San Francisco: Berrett-Koehler Publishers, 1992).

DURING THE MEETING

1. <u>Explain the purpose of the exercise and introduce the PROUDS AND SORRIES technique.</u> Consider using a 3-P STATEMENT, Technique 8, in your introduction as charted in Fig. 6-14.

2. Ask the group to <u>answer the questions, *"What are you proud about?"* and *"What are you sorry about?"*</u> Display these questions on a chart similar to Fig. 6-15.

   <u>Explain the ground rules</u> for answering the questions you have posed using Fig. 6-16, exhibiting a PROUDS AND SORRIES ground rules chart.

   Note: Unless you are an outside facilitator, remember to write your own PROUDS AND SORRIES, too. If you think you will be too rushed to do them during the meeting and facilitate the meeting as well, write them down ahead of time.

3. When everyone is finished, <u>ask the participants to bring their ideas forward and attach them to the appropriate charts</u> you have prelabeled PROUDS and SORRIES.

4. <u>Ask the group to cluster their ideas with similar ideas.</u> Split the group into two, one to cluster the PROUDS, and one to cluster the SORRIES. Allow 10 to 15 minutes for clustering. Ask the two groups to put a heading on each cluster. (See CARD CLUSTERS, Technique 31, for more information on how to cluster information.)

   Option: If your group has more than 20 people, consider asking for volunteers to cluster the information while the rest of the group takes a short break.

PROUDS AND SORRIES

Purpose:

- To articulate and learn from the best and the worst, the highs and lows of the past year.

Process:

- We will look first individually and then as a group at your PROUDS and SORRIES.
- Next we will use this information to analyze what we want to keep in the future and what we want to discard.

Payoff:

- Insights to build a stronger team.
- Information to establish realistic goals and norms for the next year.

Figure 6-14. 3P STATEMENT for PROUDS AND SORRIES.

PROUDS AND SORRIES INDIVIDUALLY

As you look back on xxx (the last year, this project, etc):

- What are you proud about?
- What are you sorry about?
- Write your ideas on sticky notes, one idea per sticky note.

10 minutes

Figure 6-15. Instructional chart for PROUDS AND SORRIES.

5. When the PROUDS and SORRIES are clustered, ask representatives from each group to read aloud all the information in each category.
6. Debrief PROUDS AND SORRIES. You might ask the group, for example,

   As you listened to the other groups, what common threads did you hear? What in particular stood out for you? What can we learn from this information?

   Option: Ask your group to create a priority list of the proudest PROUDS and the sorriest SORRIES. This list would be used to summarize the feelings of the group, and is especially helpful with large groups or groups with long lists of PROUDS AND SORRIES.
7. Use this information to establish norms, goals, and objectives for the future.

   Option: This technique is frequently followed by KEEP/THROW, Technique 47, as a tool to move toward goal setting.

PROUDS AND SORRIES GROUND RULES

1. It's ok to say what you're proud about that others did.
2. It's not ok to say what you're sorry about that others did, except for your reactions or responses to what others did, or your part in what happened. For example: I am sorry you were a jerk. (not ok) vs. I am sorry that we didn't work together better under pressure. (ok)

Figure 6-16. *Ground rules chart for* PROUDS AND SORRIES.

47

KEEP/THROW

Our group is planning for the future. We know we need to change, but some of the things we are doing are good and shouldn't be changed. Is there a technique for helping us get rid of the bad and keep the good?

What is KEEP/THROW?

KEEP/THROW is a technique that provides a process for a group to agree on what is working and should continue to be done, and what is not working and should be discontinued.

When planning for the future, radical changes are sometimes needed to meet the new goals. In this situation, some people and groups will want to throw everything on the scrap heap and start from scratch. This method definitely gets rid of the bad, but it doesn't honor or preserve what is already good. It can also leave participants feeling that everything they have done in the past was worthless. KEEP/THROW allows for a healthier, more productive approach to change that supports past successes by honoring what is good.

When do I use KEEP/THROW?

- When your group is planning for the future.
- When your group wants to identify methods to work together more effectively.
- When your group is finished with one project and beginning another.

Note: This technique is often used as a final step to PROUDS AND SORRIES, Technique 46.

How do I use KEEP/THROW?

BEFORE THE MEETING

1. Assemble enough sticky notes, marking pens, and chart paper to bring to the meeting.

2. Prepare any charts or overheads you plan to use.

DURING THE MEETING

1. Introduce the technique. You might say, for example,

SOURCE: Marvin Weisbord, *Discovering Common Ground* (San Francisco: Berrett-Koehler Publishers, 1992).

Some of what we have done in the past definitely needs to be changed. But some of what we have done has been very effective and we should keep these things. Let's use a technique called KEEP/THROW to help us differentiate between the two as a first step toward planning how to work together in the future.

2. Ask the group to individually brainstorm their answers to the following two questions on sticky notes, one answer per sticky note.

   What things are we currently doing that you would like to KEEP and carry into the future? What things are we currently doing that you would like to THROW and leave behind?

   Post a chart or overhead similar to Fig. 6-17 to support you.

3. Ask the group to bring their ideas forward and attach them to the appropriate charts you have prelabeled KEEP and THROW.

4. Ask the group to cluster their ideas with other similar ideas. Split the group into two, one to cluster KEEPs and one to cluster THROWs. Allow about 10 to 15 minutes for clustering. Ask the two groups to put a heading name on each cluster.

5. After each group is finished, ask them to review the work of the other group. When participants have read all the clusters in both the KEEP and THROW categories, ask them to sit back down.

6. Debrief the exercise with these or similar questions:

   What stands out in your mind as you read this KEEP/THROW information? What questions do you have about the work of the other groups? What were your reactions to what you read? What conclusions can we draw? What should we do with this information?

7. Incorporate the information as the group suggests based on their response to the final question, *"What shall we do with this information?"* For example, you might want to keep the lists as a reference for when the group creates goals and action plans for the future.

KEEP/THROW

1. What things are we currently doing that you would like to carry into the future?

2. What things are we currently doing that you would like to leave behind?

Write one idea per sticky note.

10 minutes

Figure 6-17. Instructions chart for KEEP/THROW.

48

WORKING BREAK

Sometimes my participants use meeting time to discuss private, one-on-one issues that don't include the rest of the group. How can I prevent this from happening?

What is WORKING BREAK?

WORKING BREAK is a technique that provides your meeting group with a designated period of time for addressing private, one-on-one issues during the meeting without wasting the time of the other participants. This is a short, informal time specifically set aside in the meeting to take care of private or small group business. It also allows for stretching and refreshing beverages.

The reality is that when colleagues get together, they tend to use the opportunity to catch up on personal pieces of business not related to the agenda at hand. Unfortunately, it is often more convenient and faster for them to take care of this business during your meeting rather than somewhere else. This behavior occurs even if it means using other people's time unwisely.

When people know that there is time set aside for their private business, they tend to stay more focused on the tasks at hand. The WORKING BREAK technique provides that time.

When do I use WORKING BREAK?

- When meeting participants come from long distances and are not able to see each other on a regular basis.
- When several group members have small pieces of one-on-one business with each other.
- When your meetings are getting sidetracked by people sharing information that is not pertinent to the entire group.

How do I use WORKING BREAK?

1. When appropriate, create a specific time during your meetings (perhaps 5 to 10 minutes) that allows individual participants or small groups to take care of their private business not related to the agenda of your meeting.

   Note: This should only be done when appropriate, i.e., when the conversations don't involve the entire group and are not using the time of the other participants wisely.

2. Post ground rules, as illustrated in Fig. 6-18.

WORKING BREAK GROUND RULES

- Avoid discussing issues relevant to entire group.
- Stick to brief issues, such as making an appointment or checking a deadline.
- Please stand up and move around the room, but stay in the room.
- Socialize if you have no relevant business. Stay available for others who might have business with you.
- If a person is engaged, stand nearby to indicate that you are waiting.
- Please return to your seats when the time has expired.

Figure 6-18. Ground rules for WORKING BREAK.

Note: Until your group is very familiar with WORKING BREAK, bring a prepared WORKING BREAK ground rules chart with you to all your meetings.

49

NEW SHOES

Participants in our meetings sometimes ask themselves "Is anybody listening?" This tends to happen especially during heated debates. How can I be sure that people are truly listening, and that everyone feels that he or she has been listened to?

What is NEW SHOES?

NEW SHOES is a technique for ensuring that people in your meeting groups are listening, understanding, and can explain the other perspectives being presented in the room. This is accomplished by asking participants to summarize what they heard to the satisfaction of the people who originally presented an idea or point of view.

This process doesn't necessarily mean the participants agree with everything that has been summarized, but is designed to ensure that people are listening and understanding.

When do I use NEW SHOES?

- When there are contentious situations in your meetings.
- When people are doing a better job at stating their side of the story than at listening to the other sides.
- When you want to reinforce to all participants that they have been listened to.

How do I use NEW SHOES?

1. Introduce NEW SHOES during a part of your meeting when it is particularly important that the opinions of all parties are understood.
2. Listen to all points of view.
3. Ask people to state what they heard from the other participants' points of view. Have them include facts and feelings. Note that they can summarize accurately without agreeing with what the other person has said. Post ground rules for this exercise similar to those shown in Fig. 6-19.
4. After the summary, ask the person whose viewpoint was being summarized to approve of the summary. That person or the facilitator can ask questions for clarification if appropriate.

   Note: Give all participants the opportunity to have their viewpoints summarized by the others in the room.

- Summarize what you heard another person say.
- Include not only facts, but also how you perceive that the other person feels about what was said.

Ground Rules:

- Honor the self-esteem and personal perspectives of the other participants.
- Use supportive vocal intonations. Sarcasm is not acceptable.
- Look at the person whose perspective you are summarizing.

Figure 6-19. Instructional and ground rules chart for NEW SHOES.

5. <u>Move forward with problem solving</u> or whatever goal you were working toward on the agenda.

    Option: When participants offer solutions, ask them to offer solutions that they believe would be acceptable to those with other opinions, as well as from their own perspectives.

50

5 WHYS

Why? Why?
Why?
Why? Why?

Sometimes I feel as though we haven't done a very good job at getting to the bottom of a problem. Is there a quick technique to identify the core cause of a relatively simple problem?

What is 5 WHYS?

5 WHYS is a technique for getting to the source of a problem in minimum time. It is said that to get to the core of a problem one will need to ask the question *"Why?"* an average of 5 times. 5 WHYS involves asking this basic question until your meeting group is satisfied that the root cause of a problem is stated and understood.

When do I use 5 WHYS?

- When you are unsure of what specifically caused a situation to be as it is.
- When you want a systematic way to lead a group to understand the real reason why a problem is occurring or has occurred.

How do I use 5 WHYS?

1. Simply <u>ask the question, *"Why?"*</u> or *"What caused that to happen?"* about the specific problem under analysis.
2. Continue to ask *"Why?"* until your meeting group feels it has <u>come to the core reason for the problem,</u> or is getting responses that seem trivial or banal. Chart the responses as appropriate.

   Note: This may involve talking to several people at several layers of the organization before the problem is fully understood.
3. <u>Use the resulting information</u> as planned.

51

SWOTs

We want to set goals but we can't agree how or where to focus our efforts. We all have our favorite areas, but there must be a better way. We need a method for gathering information so that we can get the most mileage for our efforts. What do you suggest?

Strengths
Weaknesses
Opportunities
Threats

What is SWOTs?

SWOTs is a technique for gathering information for strategic planning and other goal setting meetings. SWOT information (Strengths, Weaknesses, Opportunities, and Threats) provides data to accurately determine your group's current performance. A group can mean any organization or any team, unit, department, or division within that organization. SWOT information also provides a foundation for effectively and intelligently setting goals and priorities and making key decisions for the group's future.

Strengths and Weaknesses examine the internal environment of the group. Examples of the internal environment include: how effectively employee skills and other resources are being used; the effectiveness of technology and tracking systems; levels of creativity and risk taking; approaches to competition; and how well the organization functions as a unit.

Opportunities and Threats focus on the external environment affecting the group. The external environment can include industry, competitor, economic, social, political, and organization-specific information. Data may include potential changes in technology, products, markets, financing, raw materials, and labor; threats from new competition; bargaining power of suppliers and buyers; and customer expectations.

When do I use SWOTs?

- When an organization, or group within an organization, wants feedback on its performance.
- When your group wants to gather information before setting long- or short-term goals.

How do I use SWOTs?

BEFORE THE MEETING

1. Prepare for the SWOT analysis.

   a. Define what information should be collected.

      Some groups are very detailed in their analysis and develop a long series of specific questions. Others perform better with fewer specific questions. Determine the best approach for your group along with those participants selected to help plan your SWOT analysis.

Most groups ask four questions: What are our internal Strengths? What are our internal Weaknesses? What are our external Opportunities? What are our external Threats?

Note: Be sure to ask only OPEN-ENDED QUESTIONS. (See Technique 34 for details.)

Note: There is a danger in asking very specific questions. Specifics can influence what is considered and can narrow the potential range of responses. On the other hand, an incomplete SWOT assessment can result in a false sense of security. Do as much in-depth investigation as is feasible for your group. SWOTs should be an annual event, and the next round can be more in-depth and sophisticated, if necessary.

b. Determine who should be asked for SWOT information. Ask the group: *"Which stakeholder groups should be included? What other sources of data should be included (financial, etc.)?"*

SWOT information is gathered by asking your stakeholders a series of questions. Stakeholders include all people who have a stake in the success of the group. These people include both internal and external customers, employees from as many layers as possible within the organization, managers at all levels, suppliers, stockholders, and lenders.

Note: It is critical that information be gathered from *all* stakeholders, not just from the group that will be analyzing the information in the meeting.

Note: MINDMAPPING, Technique 29, works well to brainstorm stakeholder categories.

Note: Information on external Opportunities and Threats can also be obtained from journals, magazines, newsletters, trade shows, conventions, federal reports, and private research groups.

c. Decide how the SWOT analysis will be conducted.

SWOT questions are usually asked in face-to-face interviews or by questionnaire.

d. Determine roles, responsibilities, and time frames for collecting SWOT data.

Agree on who will be responsible for contacting stakeholders, preparing questionnaires and cover letters, memos, etc. If you are using financial or other written data, determine how and when it will be collected.

2. Gather SWOT information.

Note: If you use written questionnaires, ask people to write in complete sentences and explain themselves so the data can be clearly understood. If you are using face-to-face interviews, ask interviewers to be precise in recording responses. (See INDIVIDUAL INTERVIEWS, Technique 35, and QUESTIONNAIRES, Technique 37, for more information.)

Note: If there is a lack of trust and openness in the organization, take extra care to keep responses confidential. If people are afraid of having their handwriting recognized or E-mail messages traced, consider having participants send their SWOT comments directly to an outside facilitator.

3. <u>Compile the accumulated SWOT data for your meeting.</u>
Accumulate SWOT responses by category, one section each for Strengths, Weaknesses, Opportunities, and Threats. Each person's response should be recorded verbatim, even if there are duplicate responses. Information, if extensive, may be subdivided within each SWOT category, but there is no need to label these subdivisions at this time. Leave that for the participants.

Option: Some groups find it helpful to code the responses by stakeholder category, e.g., E = employee, M = manager, UM = upper management, C = customer, etc.

Note: Although it is an option to categorize and label SWOT information for presentation at the meeting, this is not recommended. Participants have higher ownership of SWOT data when they analyze and categorize the information themselves.

DURING THE MEETING

1. <u>Review the purpose, process, and expected payoff for the SWOT exercise</u> (see 3P STATEMENTS, Technique 8). For example:
The purpose of today's meeting is to analyze our SWOT data, and use it as a basis for setting our group's goals for the next two years. After our analysis, we will identify ways to maximize our strengths and opportunities and minimize our weaknesses and threats. This process will focus our efforts for improving our competitiveness.

2. <u>Break participants into four groups,</u> one group to analyze Strengths, another for Weaknesses, another group for Opportunities, and the fourth group for Threats.

Option: If each group has more than eight people, consider creating two or more groups for Strengths, two groups for Weaknesses, et cetera.

Option: Consider using preassigned groups to ensure a mixture of opinions and levels of the organization. (See SMALL GROUPS, Technique 20, for details.)

3. <u>Give the groups specific exercise instructions.</u> Post a chart with instructions, such as those in Fig. 6-20, as a visual aid.

a. Ask each group to pick a reporter, recorder, and timekeeper. (See SELF-MANAGEMENT, Technique 10, for details.)

b. Ask each group to read the information on their area (Strengths, Weaknesses, Opportunities, or Threats).

SWOT Small Group Instructions

1. Introduce yourselves. Pick a recorder, a reporter, and a timekeeper.

   2 minutes

2. Individually read the information on your area of expertise.

   15 minutes

3. When everyone is ready, categorize the information.

   15 minutes

   Use short phrases to describe categories. Be specific.

   Total time: 32 minutes

Figure 6-20. Small group instructions for SWOTs.

> *Note:* Later, you can provide the raw data for all SWOT categories for any-one who is interested. For now participants are to read only their section.

> *Note:* To determine how much time is appropriate for this exercise, read a section closely and time yourself.

c. After all individuals in each group have finished reading the information in their SWOT section, ask each group to categorize their information into head-ings with short phrases. For example: The Strengths group might identify "skilled employees" instead of "employees." The Weaknesses group might identify "overworked employees." This avoids later confusion. When in doubt, participants should create two categories instead of one. For in-stance, "skilled and dedicated employees" should be broken down into two categories. The recorder should write each category on a flip chart, leaving substantial space between categories for the next exercise.

> *Note:* This section should take approximately 20 minutes for every 10 pages of data. If the groups need more or less time, adjust ac-cordingly.

4. Ask the small group reporters to succinctly summarize their group's results for the rest of the participants. Leave time for questions or additions from other groups, but keep the report session snappy to maintain the group's energy. Fig-ure 6-21 illustrates the instructions.

> *Option:* If you have more than one group looking at each area (Strengths, Weak-nesses, etc.) have those subgroups meet first and combine their infor-mation. This will probably take from 15 to 25 minutes. Then move to the reporting session, step 4. Figure 6-22 illustrates those instructions.

5. As a group, review the results of your SWOT analysis. Lead a group discussion. For example:

```
┌──────────────────────────────────────────────────────┐
│                                                        │
│                    REPORT BACK                         │
│                                                        │
│   Please give us a succinct report of the categories your group found. │
│                                          10 minutes per group │
│                                                        │
│   We will leave a few minutes for questions at the end. │
│                                           5 minutes per group │
│                                                        │
└──────────────────────────────────────────────────────┘
```

Figure 6-21. Instructions chart for SWOT report back.

What are your reactions to the results of our SWOT analysis? What in particular stands out for you? What did you find surprising/not surprising? What should we do with this information? (If not already planned.)

Summarize the group's discussion and subsequent plans for using this information.

```
┌──────────────────────────────────────────────────────┐
│                                                        │
│            SUBGROUP CONSOLIDATION (IF NECESSARY)       │
│                                                        │
│   Pick a recorder, reporter, and timekeeper for your new combined group. │
│                                               1 minute │
│                                                        │
│   Each subgroup gives a 10 minute (or less) report on their group's │
│   categories.                                          │
│                                             10 minutes │
│                                                        │
│   Combine lists. Recorder creates a new list, or makes revisions on existing │
│   lists.                                               │
│                                             10 minutes │
│                                    Total time: 21 minutes │
│                                                        │
└──────────────────────────────────────────────────────┘
```

Figure 6-22. Instructions chart for SWOT subgroup consolidation.

7

11 Techniques to Make Decisions

When it comes to making decisions, Roberta's Board of Directors take forever.

They hem and haw, analyze and reanalyze. They debate and debate and then they debate some more. Even the simplest decisions can take hours. I know I'm not using their time wisely, but what can I do to help?

Making decisions is a key activity in today's participative meetings. Once a problem has been defined and analyzed and the potential solutions brainstormed, decisions must be made. How can a meeting group or organization improve the quality of their decision making and do so with a minimum amount of stress? This chapter provides eleven techniques to ensure that the best decisions are made, that the decisions are understood and agreed upon by everyone, and that when multiple decisions are made, they are prioritized for the most effective implementation.

Techniques are:

- 52 VROOM YETTON DECISION-MAKING MODEL
- 53 MULTIVOTING
- 54 NEGATIVE VOTING
- 55 DOTS
- 56 100 VOTES

- 57 NOMINAL PRIORITIZATION
- 58 3 FOR/3 AGAINST
- 59 IDEA SWAP
- 60 CRITERIA MATRIX
- 61 IMPACT AND CHANGEABILITY ANALYSIS
- 62 FORCE FIELD ANALYSIS

52

VROOM YETTON DECISION-MAKING MODEL

I'm all for participation, but sometimes it doesn't seem logical that every decision should be made as a group. It's overkill and sometimes the payoff is marginal. Is there a technique that will help our organization to determine effectively the most appropriate person or group to make each decision we are confronted with?

What is VROOM YETTON DECISION-MAKING MODEL?

The VROOM YETTON DECISION-MAKING MODEL is a technique for determining how much participation is needed or desired to make a specific decision. Even in this age of participation, not every decision should be made participatively. The most appropriate level of decision making depends on the specific issue and situation.

The VROOM YETTON DECISION-MAKING MODEL offers a spectrum of decision-making choices that range from authoritarian to consultative to group participation. Traditionally, a manager or group leader uses the VROOM YETTON DECISION-MAKING MODEL to decide individually how to make a given decision. The following instructions illustrate how a meeting group can use this model to determine the most appropriate level of participation for any decision facing them.

When do I use VROOM YETTON DECISION-MAKING MODEL?

- When the appropriate level of participation in making a specific decision is not clear.
- When you are not sure if a specific issue is worthy of meeting time.

How do I use VROOM YETTON DECISION-MAKING MODEL?

1. <u>Articulate the decision or decisions to be made.</u>
2. <u>Outline the VROOM YETTON DECISION-MAKING MODEL</u> to your meeting group. Vroom and Yetton, the creators of this model, identified five distinct methods for making decisions. These methods are categorized as illustrated in Fig. 7-1. In this figure, A stands for Authoritarian, C for Consultative, and G for Group.
3. <u>Lead a group discussion on how to address the decisions under consideration</u> based on the choices displayed in Fig. 7-1.

SOURCE: Victor Vroom and Philip Yetton, *Leadership and Decision-Making* (Pittsburgh: University of Pittsburgh Press, 1973).

VROOM YETTON DECISION-MAKING MODEL

A1 Leader makes decision alone without input.

A2 Leader informally requests information from employees, then makes decision alone.

C1 Leader formally requests information or opinions from employees in one-on-one meetings, then makes decision alone.

C2 Leader holds group meeting to discuss the issue, then makes decision alone.

G2 Leader holds group meeting to discuss the issue and group makes the decision.

Figure 7-1. The VROOM YETTON DECISION-MAKING MODEL.

4. After the discussion, <u>ask the participants to vote for what they each consider to be the best choice within the model for the specific decisions to be made.</u> Have them make tick marks on a prepared chart similar to Fig. 7-2.

   Option: Provide each participant with a preprepared voting ballot so that each participant can vote privately.

   Option: Vote by computer.

5. <u>Proceed accordingly.</u> Create a communication plan, including time frames, especially if the entire meeting group is not involved in making the decision.

   Note: Note the possible irony in participatively deciding to take a nonparticipative decision. However, there is equal irony in deciding in an authoritarian style to take a participative decision. Even if the group decides that the decision is best made authoritatively, this is a good way to get agreement on the best way to proceed. Leaders may be surprised at what their employees think should be their realm.

HOW SHOULD THIS DECISION BE MADE?

A1 _____   A2 _____   C1 _____   C2 _____   G2 _____

Please come forward and place a tick mark next to the method that you think is most appropriate for making this decision.

Figure 7-2. VROOM YETTON voting chart.

53

MULTIVOTING

After we brainstorm, it almost always takes too long to narrow down our options to a few of the most realistic ideas for discussion. What can we do to save time in this situation?

What is MULTIVOTING?

MULTIVOTING is a technique for narrowing a wide range of ideas or choices down to the few most appropriate, feasible, and important. This technique saves time while still allowing consideration of every idea that has been generated.

While MULTIVOTING is not a technique for making a single, specific decision, it is a fabulous technique for prioritizing large amounts of information without losing energy or wasting time.

When do I use MULTIVOTING?

- When your group has to narrow down a range of alternatives for closer analysis.
- When a selection or prioritization step is necessary after brainstorming.

How do I use MULTIVOTING?

1. Brainstorm your subject or issue, recording all ideas.

   Note: See THE OLD-FASHIONED WAY, Technique 28, or NOMINAL GROUP PROCESS, Technique 43, for details.

2. Briefly review each brainstormed idea to make sure that everyone understands it. Allow a one-minute explanation for any ideas that need explanation.

   Note: Remember not to allow any analysis or criticism of the ideas at this point.

3. When all the ideas are clear, ask your participants to vote by a show of hands for all issues which they believe are worthy of further discussion.

   Note: At this point there is no cap on the number of ideas each person can vote for.

   Option: Ask the participants to come forward and place ticks by all ideas on the brainstorming chart that they feel are worthy of further discussion. If you are going to use this option, create a designated area adjacent to each idea so it is easy to count the number of tick marks.

4. <u>Tabulate the votes. Any issue that receives at least half of all possible votes remains in contention for the next round of voting.</u> For example, if a total of twenty people are voting, any one idea must receive at least ten votes to remain in contention. Circle or otherwise distinguish each of the ideas that pass this test, and count the total number of ideas still remaining on the list.

   Note: Although the other ideas are shelved at this time, let the group know that you will keep the complete list available for review and consideration again at a later date. This avoids any potential rework if the group needs to analyze more ideas in the future.

5. <u>Ask your participants to vote again, but this time for only the top half of the remaining ideas.</u> In other words, if there are twenty-four remaining ideas, each person gets twelve votes.

   Note: Vote using the same method as before, either by a raise of hands or with tick marks.

6. After the second round of voting is completed, <u>continue voting</u> as outlined in Steps 4 and 5 <u>until the group arrives at what they consider to be an appropriate number of ideas for further analysis.</u>

   Note: An appropriate number is typically from three to five remaining ideas. It is possible that the group could arrive at this number after Step 3 or after one round of Steps 4 and 5.

   Note: MULTIVOTING is not a technique for choosing one option. Using it for that purpose would create a false sense of consensus. Don't narrow your choices down below three before beginning more in-depth analysis.

7. <u>Discuss and analyze the remaining ideas at length.</u>

   Option: Analyze each idea together as a group, either in small or large group discussions.

   Option: Create task force groups to research each idea. Then establish a time and date for the whole group to discuss the ideas again.

8. <u>Proceed with appropriate next steps.</u>

54

NEGATIVE VOTING

A majority of our group generally agrees which solutions are best without too many problems. But sometimes I'm not so sure we are in complete harmony. Is there a simple technique that will help ensure that we have full consensus?

What is NEGATIVE VOTING?

NEGATIVE VOTING is a technique that identifies which people do *not* support a proposed decision, instead of those who do.

By identifying those who don't support a given decision, the meeting group can talk to those people, discover their specific concerns, and identify methods to alleviate these concerns. By doing so, it is possible to gain consensus among the group before moving forward. This is an excellent way to proactively prevent problems before they occur.

When do I use NEGATIVE VOTING?

- When you want to make a decision by consensus.
- When you need to decide among a few difficult choices.
- When you want to enhance the acceptability of your decisions.
- When group members might be pressured to agree with the majority.

How do I use NEGATIVE VOTING?

1. <u>After adequate discussion and analysis</u> concerning a specific decision or option under consideration, <u>ask your meeting group, *"Who cannot live with this option?"* Count and chart the number of people who raise their hands.</u> Ask the same question for all options being considered by the group.

2. After this process, identify which options have accumulated the lowest number of negative votes. Obtain permission from the group to <u>eliminate the options with the highest number of negative votes.</u>

3. Taking one option at a time, <u>ask each dissenting voter what concerns they have about the remaining options.</u> Chart their concerns. Leave ample chart space between each listed concern because it will be utilized in the next step.

4. When finished, ask the entire group to <u>brainstorm ideas that will alleviate the listed concerns.</u> For example:

Who can think of a way to alleviate this problem for Harold? or *What ideas do you have to alleviate this list of concerns about Option One?*

Document all ideas in the spaces between each listed concern on your chart.

Note: Use a different color pen to distinguish between the concerns and the brainstormed ideas.

Note: If you haven't left sufficient room to write on your existing chart, create a new chart for the ideas brainstormed. Be sure to clearly label which ideas go with which concerns.

Note: If necessary, remind the group of the rules for brainstorming.

5. After you are finished brainstorming, <u>ask each "dissenter" if the group's suggested changes now allow them to support the option.</u> For example:

What do you think, Harold? How do these ideas work for you? Do they provide enough information or changes so that you can support this option?

Note: If you are voting on more than one option, ask these questions for all of the options.

6. <u>Do a second negative vote.</u> *"Who cannot support Option One when it includes these changes?"*

Note: If appropriate, paraphrase the changes that were suggested.

Note: It is unlikely that all options will still receive negative votes, but if this does happen, discuss with the group how to handle the situation. You may want to repeat Steps 3, 4, and 5, or you may decide to brainstorm new, more creative ideas.

7. If more than one option remains that everyone supports, <u>follow up with a positive vote</u> to ascertain which choice is best. You might introduce this by asking, for example, *"Which of these two choices do you think is best?"*

55

DOTS

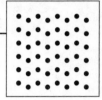

There are times when we need a quick read on our initial reactions to potential decisions. Is there a technique I can use to accomplish this?

What is DOTS?

DOTS is a technique for visually ascertaining a meeting group's immediate reactions to proposed solutions or goals.

DOTS can be especially effective when you want to accurately capture the personal sentiments of everyone within your meeting group. This is a quick and easy decision-making technique that can keep the process of decision making fun, yet effective.

When do I use DOTS?

- When you want to ensure that everyone's opinions are considered.
- When you want to gain feedback on the group's opinions in a short amount of time.
- When you have completed a goal-setting or action-planning discussion.

How do I use DOTS?

BEFORE THE MEETING

1. You will need to <u>purchase enough colored dots for the exercise.</u> These can typically be purchased at minimal cost at many office supply stores.

   Note: Be sure to buy dots that are large enough to be seen from across a large room.

   Option: If dots aren't available, purchase stars instead.

2. <u>Prepare any chart or overhead you plan to use.</u>

DURING THE MEETING

1. After brainstormed ideas have been discussed and clarified, <u>ask the group to come forward and "dot vote" for every idea under consideration.</u> You might say in explanation, for example,

   Using these color-coded dots will give us an indication of which ideas are agreed upon, which have no support, and which need further discussion.

   Use a chart or overhead, as illustrated in Fig. 7-3, to support your instructions.

DOT VOTE

- Vote for all ideas.
- One dot per idea.
- Vote with the dot that best communicates your opinion.

Green Dot = Yes, I support this.

Red Dot = No, I do not support this.

Yellow Dot = I am neutral on this.

Black Dot = I need more information before I can make a decision.

Total time: 10 minutes

Figure 7-3. Instruction chart for DOTS.

Option: Depending on the situation, you might want to use only red and green dots.

2. <u>After the "dot vote," ask the group for their feedback</u> using OPEN-ENDED QUESTIONS, Technique 34. You might say, for example,

What stands out for you? What are your reactions to what you see? What conclusions can we draw from our dot vote? What are the logical next steps?

3. <u>Summarize</u> all the information from the DOTS exercise and move on accordingly.

56

100 VOTES

The groups I facilitate often need to prior-itize their ideas. It would be helpful to understand where the group's true energy and priorities are so that our decisions are more likely to be implemented. Is there a technique I can use to accomplish this?

What is 100 VOTES?

There are times when all meeting groups need to establish what their priorities are. 100 VOTES is a technique for determining a group's preferences among a number of different ideas or potential choices.

100 VOTES involves each participant distributing a total of 100 VOTES among the available choices presented. The resulting information can then be used to make decisions about what projects to take on, which ideas to pursue, what direction to go, or which actions to take. This is a very effective decision-making technique, as it reveals what a group will most likely support.

When do I use 100 VOTES?

- When you want to create a short list of priorities.
- When you need to know where the group's energy is regarding a number of ideas.

How do I use 100 VOTES?

1. After a number of potential options, goals, or actions have been identified, charted, and clarified, <u>allot meeting participants 100 votes each, which they can allocate to this list according to their priorities.</u> To explain the technique, you might say, for example,

   Now we're going to prioritize the ideas we have generated using a tech-nique called 100 VOTES. You each have 100 VOTES to allocate among what you believe to be the best ideas. In this case, the best ideas are the ones that you have energy around or would give priority to. There are also very likely some ideas that you might think don't deserve any effort or consid-eration. Don't give any votes to those. There may be one, two, or more that you think are fantastic ideas. You will probably want to designate the majority of your votes to those. And there may be some ideas that you think have some merit which deserve some attention. Place the rest of your votes with those. But remember that you only have 100 VOTES. The point of the exercise is to use your votes in a way that accurately weights your individual priorities regarding the ideas we are considering.

Note: All the potential choices need to be posted on chart paper around the room so that all participants will be able to cast their votes easily. The participants should write directly on the charts the number of votes they wish to allocate to each option.

2. <u>Tally the votes and display a summary</u> for each choice with the number of people voting and number of votes cast for each issue. For example, 5/58 means five members cast a total of 58 votes.

3. Ask your participants to take a few minutes to visually <u>review the data</u> they have just generated.

4. <u>Ask the group for their reactions.</u> You might ask, for example,

   What are your reactions to what you see? What surprises you? What questions or concerns do you have?

5. <u>Decide as a group which issues to focus on and which to put aside.</u>

6. <u>Create an action plan</u> as appropriate.

57

NOMINAL PRIORITIZATION

Our group is usually able to generate a list of goals and actions very easily. But after our meetings, we find that we are over our heads with too much extra work. As a result, nothing gets done. Is there a technique that will help us prioritize our ideas so that we spend our time on only the most important issues?

What is NOMINAL PRIORITIZATION?

NOMINAL PRIORITIZATION is a technique for measuring and thereby identifying the priority of issues, decisions, or action plans.

The demands placed on organizations today are such that not all issues can be given equal consideration. Even in ideal situations, some issues are simply more important to a group or organization than others and need to be given top priority.

NOMINAL PRIORITIZATION quickly and accurately reveals a meeting group's actual priorities.

When do I use NOMINAL PRIORITIZATION?

- When the group cannot accomplish everything and must set priorities.
- After a list of goals or objectives has been created, and priorities must be established.

How do I use NOMINAL PRIORITIZATION?

1. <u>After brainstorming a complete list of issues, ideas, goals, or actions, ask your meeting group for help in prioritizing these choices.</u>

   Note: All choices must be visually displayed for the group on chart paper or a computer screen. When using chart paper, be sure to create enough voting space for each choice.

   Ask each person to rank each item under consideration using the following ratings:

   1 = most importance or impact

   2 = medium importance or impact

   3 = least importance or impact

   All choices can theoretically be given the same rating. This is not to be considered a forced ranking decision. Use Fig. 7-4 as a visual aid for your instructions.

Figure 7-4. NOMINAL PRIORITIZATION rating instructions.

> *Note:* Have participants give their rankings by private ballot, finger count, or by any other logical and efficient voting technique.

> *Note:* Remember that you should also vote unless you are an outside, neutral facilitator.

2. After everyone is finished with their ratings, <u>determine the average for each choice</u> by adding up the scores for that choice and dividing the total by the number of persons voting. Ask the group to help you with this by delegating a few of the options to each person in the group. Ask them to round to the nearest tenth. For example, 1.67 becomes 1.7 and 2.23 becomes 2.2.

> *Note:* Be sure that each group writes the average or mean for each choice in large enough numbers to be seen by everyone in the group.

> *Note:* It is a good idea to bring hand-held calculators to distribute for use.

3. <u>Ask the group for their reactions</u> to the prioritized rankings.

4. <u>Ask the group to agree how to prioritize the issues</u> based on the results of the rating process. You might ask, for example,

What decisions seem logical based on the results of this exercise? Which options should we choose? What level of priority should we seek to achieve (only address issues with group priority ratings of 1.0, 1.5, etc.)?

> *Note:* Most groups will drop the items with the lowest ratings, or put them aside for discussion at a later date. Allow time for lobbying if necessary and decide as a group how to handle any issues of disagreement.

5. <u>Create action plans</u> for all issues selected by the group as priorities.

58

3 FOR / 3 AGAINST

Because all sides of an issue don't get equal air time, the most vocal and opinionated people in my group always seem to get their way. Is there a technique that can help me alleviate this problem?

What is 3 FOR / 3 AGAINST?

3 FOR / 3 AGAINST is a technique for assuring that all sides of an issue are heard.

By design, 3 FOR / 3 AGAINST asks for both the pros and the cons for every option or issue being discussed. This insures that any decisions to be made are based on all of the information available, not just the opinions of the most vocal contingents.

When do I use 3 FOR / 3 AGAINST?

- When you want to be sure that all sides of an issue get equal time.
- When you are planning to present an idea for approval.

How do I use 3 FOR / 3 AGAINST?

1. Introduce the 3 FOR / 3 AGAINST technique and describe how it will be used in your meeting. You might say, for example,

   It is important that we hear all sides of all available options before we can decide on the right option for us. In the past, we have not done a very good job of this. Today let's try a new technique which will ensure that both sides of the issue are discussed. It's called 3 FOR / 3 AGAINST. When we discuss an issue, please note that for every three comments we hear in support of an option, we will also generate three comments against that option. These 3 FOR and 3 AGAINST can be offered by one person or by any of you within the group. Three is an arbitrary number. The point is to systematically hear both sides of the issue. What do you think about our using 3 FOR / 3 AGAINST in our meeting today?

   Note: Your group may feel that always sticking to the number 3 is limiting and inappropriate. Be flexible. Remember that in the final analysis, the primary goal of this process is to elicit comments on both sides of an issue.

2. When an issue is being discussed, ask your group to provide three reasons why the issue should be supported, and then three reasons why it should not be supported. If you are discussing many options use the technique for each option.

3. After the discussion, ask your participants to decide upon the best option for the group.

   Option: You can employ any of the voting techniques to aid you at this point. See NEGATIVE VOTING, Technique 54; DOTS, Technique 55; or 100 VOTES, Technique 56.

59

IDEA SWAP

Some of the ideas from one group are not always welcomed or advocated by other groups within the same organization. What can I do to stimulate agreement and verify that there is support among groups before too much work has gone into a specific idea?

What is IDEA SWAP?

IDEA SWAP is a technique that both identifies and builds ideas that have the most support.

This process involves a group trading their ideas with another group to get reactions, modifications, and approval. Ideas that will be widely supported quickly emerge. Receiving input in the embryo or planning stages increases teamwork, builds stronger ideas, and improves commitment to implementation.

IDEA SWAP can be used among peer groups or between different levels of management, and helps insure that decisions are endorsed and supported by all.

When do I use IDEA SWAP?

- When defining the future direction, goals, or implementation plans of a group.
- When deciding which options should be selected.
- When widespread support of any idea is essential.
- After a large meeting group has narrowed down a list of goals or ideas and is creating specific implementation plans in smaller work groups.

How do I use IDEA SWAP?

1. After a short list of goals or ideas has been identified, <u>break the meeting participants into smaller groups.</u> The number of groups should match the number of issues to be addressed. You may <u>assign issues to groups</u> or ask for volunteers for each topic. <u>Ask each group to draft its ideas or specific actions for addressing its issue.</u> Have each group outline these ideas in enough detail to be understood by the other groups.

   Note: Plan detailed instructions for this step and chart them. These instructions will vary depending on your situation. See SMALL GROUPS, Technique 20, or GOAL PLAN GO, Technique 65, for ideas if needed. Allow at least 20 minutes for this step, possibly much more depending on the complexity of each topic.

2. <u>Have each group pass its ideas on to another group for analysis and further consideration.</u> For example, ask each group to pass its ideas to the group on its immediate left.

3. <u>Ask each group to review the new information.</u> Allow the groups to build and modify these ideas or actions into a form that is acceptable to them. Display the instructions and guidelines for IDEA SWAP as shown in Fig. 7-5.

IDEA SWAP

1. Choose a recorder, a reporter, and a timekeeper.

1 minute

2. Review the ideas or actions. Be sure everyone understands each point.

10 minutes

3. Chart the pros and cons.

15 minutes

4. Agree on what the group supports and does not support. Make modifications or enhancements as needed.

20 minutes

5. Create a chart outlining the ideas or actions your group supports

5 minutes

6. Plan to present the supported or modified ideas or actions to the rest of the group.

4 minutes

Total time: 55 minutes

Figure 7-5. IDEA SWAP instructions and guidelines.

4. <u>Ask each group to report back</u> briefly to the larger group on which ideas or actions they endorse.

5. Based on this feedback, <u>determine as a group which ideas or actions are approved for implementation.</u>

Option: Consider using 100 VOTES, Technique 56, or NOMINAL PRIORITIZATION, Technique 57.

6. <u>Create additional action plans</u> or next steps as appropriate.

Option: IDEA SWAP can also be used for swapping ideas among groups or teams that are not together in one place at one time. Plan how to have those groups communicate with each other.

60

CRITERIA MATRIX

I want to make sure that the groups I facilitate are making sound decisions based on relevant criteria, not just on the whims and fancies of the moment. Often I think this is just a matter of better organization and focus. What do you suggest?

Criteria	Choice One	Choice Two	Choice Three
Total number of Ys			

What is CRITERIA MATRIX?

CRITERIA MATRIX is a technique designed to prioritize a group of potential alternatives under consideration. This is accomplished by identifying and weighing criteria against each of those alternatives. Establishing criteria forces a group to articulate and examine their values, judgments, and assumptions before making their decision.

Criteria are standards from which one makes judgments or decisions, and their identification becomes the basis for evaluation. For example, if your work group wants to buy a specific piece of equipment and you have a maximum of $20,000 to spend, this amount is one criterion. Any equipment costing over that amount does not meet your criterion and therefore you would likely not choose it. Once all the criteria for the equipment you want to purchase are identified and agreed upon (cost, specifications, quality, warranties, maintenance schedules, etc.) your group can investigate the alternatives more objectively.

It is much easier to reach consensus when making a decision if the criteria are identified and agreed upon beforehand. People are much more willing to give up their favorite choices when they see that these favorites don't meet the necessary criteria. If there is no agreement on the criteria it is unlikely that there will be agreement on the best alternative.

It is important to recognize that not all criteria are of equal importance. Specific situations will call for weighing criteria differently. Consequently, three CRITERIA MATRIX variations will be described.

It is important to recognize that CRITERIA MATRIX does not directly result in a specific decision. Instead, it provides a visual rating of alternatives against established criteria. This data will help you focus your final discussions, in which you will identify the final decision that everyone supports.

SOURCE for Variation 2: William Daniels, *Group Power* (San Diego: Pfeiffer and Company, 1986).
SOURCE for Variation 3: Caryn Spain, Applied Business Solutions, Seattle, WA.

When do I use CRITERIA MATRIX?

- When a decision has many components or criteria which must be factored.
- When a potential decision is going around in circles without resolve.
- When several opinions and perspectives must be considered.
- When it is difficult to choose among many options or alternatives to make a decision.

How do I use CRITERIA MATRIX?

BEFORE THE MEETING

Prepare a chart or overhead for the CRITERIA MATRIX you plan to use in your meeting. If you are not sure which CRITERIA MATRIX is most appropriate for your group, prepare charts for all three variations. Refer to Figs. 7-6, 7-7, and 7-8 for templates.

DURING THE MEETING

1. Brainstorm all options to a specific problem or situation. Create a short list of serious contenders.

   Note: You could use MULTIVOTING, Technique 53, to arrive at a short list of options.

2. Brainstorm and identify all criteria to be satisfied in making the best decision for the problem or situation under consideration. Include criteria from all stakeholders, in addition to any emotional and seemingly illogical criteria.

   Note: A stakeholder is defined as anyone who has a stake in the end result or anyone who will be impacted by the decision to be made.

   Note: If necessary, help the group understand what criteria are by asking them some open-ended questions. You might ask, for example,

   What are the qualities or attributes of a good solution? What distinguishes between a good and a bad alternative in your mind? What standards does an alternative have to meet in order to be acceptable?

3. After brainstorming all criteria go back through your list to verify that all are understood. Eliminate any duplications.

4. Introduce the CRITERIA MATRIX you have selected to use for this meeting. Variation 1 functions best when all criteria have basically the same weight and the decision is not terribly complex. Use Variation 2 when clear veto criteria exist. Variation 3 is the best choice when no veto criteria exist, the decision is quite complex, and criteria vary widely in importance.

   Note: You might ask your meeting group to participate in the selection of which CRITERIA MATRIX to use.

5. Rate the short list of choices against the criteria using one of the three following variations:

	Choice One	Choice Two	Choice Three
Criteria			
Total number of Ys			

Figure 7-6. CRITERIA MATRIX for Variation 1.

VARIATION 1. Refer to Fig. 7-6.

a. List the criteria down the left side of the chart.

b. List your potential choices across the top.

c. Analyze each choice against each criterion. If the criterion is met, mark a Y for yes in the box. If the criterion is not met, mark the box with an N for no.

d. Count the number of Ys for each choice. Write that number in the space provided at the bottom of the chart.

VARIATION 2

a. Create three categories for the criteria, as illustrated in Fig. 7-7, and list the criteria based on these categories down the left side of the chart.

(1) The "Must Have" section: If these criteria are not met, the choice is immediately dropped, as noted by the VETO in the Weight section along the top of the chart.

(2) The "Important to Have" section: Failure to meet these criteria is important, but not so important as to veto the choice. Note that these criteria are weighted "times 2," double the weight of the next category.

(3) The "Would Like to Have" section: These criteria are important enough for mention, but not as important as the other two categories, as suggested by the "times 1" weighting.

List of Criteria	Criteria Weight	Option One		Option Two		Option Three	
"Must Have" Criteria							
	VETO						
	VETO						
	VETO						
"Important to Have" Criteria		Rate 1-10	Multiply × 2	Rate 1-10	Multiply × 2	Rate 1-10	Multiply × 2
	× 2	/		/		/	
	× 2	/		/		/	
	× 2	/		/		/	
	× 2	/		/		/	
"Would Like to Have" Criteria		Rate 1-10	Multiply × 1	Rate 1-10	Multiply × 1	Rate 1-10	Multiply × 1
	× 1	/		/		/	
	× 1	/		/		/	
	× 1	/		/		/	
Totals							

Figure 7-7. CRITERIA MATRIX for Variation 2.

b. <u>List your brainstormed choices</u> along the top of the chart.

c. <u>Compare each potential choice against all the selected criteria.</u>

    (1) If a choice doesn't meet a veto criteria, it is dropped from further consideration.

    (2) In the "times 2" weighting section, apply a numerical rating from 1 to 10 to show how well the group believes that the option meets the specific criterion: 1 would indicate that the option poorly meets that criterion; 5 would indicate that it satisfactorily meets the criterion; ten would mean that the criterion was exceeded. Write those numbers on the left side of the column.

    (3) In the "times 1" weighting section, apply the same numerical rating from 1 to 10 to show how well the group believes that the option meets the criteria. Write those numbers on the left side of the column.

d. Multiply all choices that weren't vetoed by their weighting factor. Place the resulting number on the right side of the appropriate box.

e. Add all the resulting factored numbers for each choice at the bottom of each column to arrive at a final rating.

VARIATION 3

a. <u>List the criteria</u> down the left side of the chart as illustrated in Fig. 7-8.

b. Have the group <u>rate the importance of each of these criteria</u> on a scale of 1 (low or not important) to 10 (high or very important).

Note: More than one criterion could receive the same rating.

c. <u>List your brainstormed choices</u> along the top of the chart.

d. <u>Weigh each choice against each of the criteria</u> on a scale of 1 (low in meeting this criterion) to 10 (high in meeting this criterion). Write this number in the left side of the column for each choice.

Criteria List All Criteria Below	Weigh the Importance of Each Criterion 1-10: 1= low, 10=high	Option One: Rate 1-10 / Multiply × weight	Option Two: Rate 1-10 / Multiply × weight	Option Three: Rate 1-10 / Multiply × weight
		/	/	/
		/	/	/
		/	/	/
		/	/	/
		/	/	/
		/	/	/
		/	/	/
		/	/	/
		/	/	/
		/	/	/
		/	/	/
		/	/	/
Totals				

Figure 7-8. CRITERIA MATRIX for Variation 3.

Note: When there is controversy about a rating, take the time to understand the points of all participants. Sometimes your group will need to further clarify the meaning of a specific criterion or the components of a specific choice. Once all opinions are understood, look for a number that all participants can support. This is usually the mean number.

  e. <u>Multiply the weight of each criterion by the weight given to each choice,</u> and write the resulting number in the right side of the appropriate column.

  f. <u>Add the resulting numbers together</u> and write the totals at the appropriate location at the bottom of the chart.

Note: For all choices, please modify the CRITERIA MATRIX grids based on the number of criteria and choices your group will analyze.

6. Using the completed CRITERIA MATRIX, <u>analyze the results as a group.</u> Use this as data for helping the group to <u>make the final decision.</u>

Note: The CRITERIA MATRIX only provides information. It does not make a decision. Your meeting group must use this data to help them make the right decision. It is possible, although not probable, that groups will make a decision different from the option supported by the CRITERIA MATRIX.

Note: If none of the options ranked well against the criteria, your group may need to consider going back to the drawing board.

61

IMPACT AND CHANGEABILITY ANALYSIS

Sometimes our group makes decisions to pursue things that we later find don't make a lot of difference, or could make a difference but are out of our control. How can we avoid these problems?

What is IMPACT AND CHANGEABILITY ANALYSIS?

IMPACT AND CHANGEABILITY ANALYSIS is a decision-making technique that helps a meeting group to isolate and focus on the options that will have the most impact on their organizational goals. In addition, this technique identifies the options that are within their authority to change.

The results of this technique are increased efficiency of effort and improved implementation.

When do I use IMPACT AND CHANGEABILITY ANALYSIS?

- When your group must choose among options.
- When not all options under consideration will have high impact on organizational goals.
- When not all options under consideration are within the control of the group.

How do I use IMPACT AND CHANGEABILITY ANALYSIS?

1. After your group has brainstormed a list of options, goals, or solutions to a problem, <u>introduce IMPACT AND CHANGEABILITY ANALYSIS and describe its purpose.</u> You might say, for example,

   In order to make sure that any actions we take will have a significant impact and also that they are within our control to change, let's use a technique called IMPACT AND CHANGEABILITY ANALYSIS to help us focus our efforts. What do you think?

2. Ask the group to <u>rate each of the proposed options</u> on a scale of one to ten, for each of the two following variables:

   a. High or low impact on the business. You might ask, for example,

   If this option is successfully implemented, will the impact on the business be high or low? Which number between one and ten seems most appropriate?

   b. High or low level of changeability.

   Does our group have a high or low level of authority in fixing this problem? If it is well within our control, we would rate it high; if it is not, we would rate it low. What number between one and ten seems most appropriate here?

Assign each option a specific letter (A, B, C, etc.) for identification so that it can be recognized easily when plotted on a preprepared chart or overhead similar to the one illustrated in Fig. 7-9.

3. Once the group has identified the numerical rating for each of the two variables, plot the group's rating on the IMPACT AND CHANGEABILITY chart. Do this for each option.

4. After all the options have been plotted on your chart, analyze the results as a group. You might ask, for example, *"What conclusions can we draw from what you see? What seem to be the logical options on which to focus our energy?"*

5. Decide as a group where to focus your energy and efforts. Create action plans to support implementation.

Note: See the other decision-making techniques described in Chap. 8, "7 Techniques to Implement Decisions," to support you.

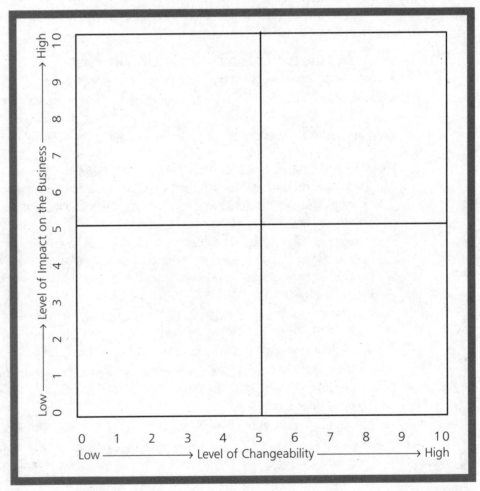

Figure 7-9. IMPACT AND CHANGEABILITY chart.

62

FORCE FIELD ANALYSIS

There are a number of competing groups within my organization. Sometimes a good idea can be squelched because the people who thought of and developed the idea did not consider its potential opposition. Is there a systematic process to deal with this type of potential problem?

What is FORCE FIELD ANALYSIS?

FORCE FIELD ANALYSIS is a technique for identifying, analyzing, and proactively addressing the opposing forces that exist for any desired change. This involves both isolating the forces that support and resist this change, and applying a process for strengthening the positive forces and weakening the negative forces so that the change can be implemented.

Forces can be powerful influencers within your own group, your organization, or your industry. In this situation they can include tangible items such as budgets, physical restrictions, and personnel, as well as intangible items such as politics, feelings, and attitudes.

As any arm wrestler knows, when two competing forces work against each other, the force which is strongest and endures the longest is the force that wins. And in the case of organizations, competing forces can be strong enough to kill even the best ideas. Your group must be prepared with processes to strengthen the forces which support a desired change so that it can become a reality.

When do I use FORCE FIELD ANALYSIS?

- When an idea is likely to face opposition.
- When your group wants to test the pros and cons of a decision before presentation to upper management or other decision makers.
- When you want to increase the likelihood that goals will be implemented.

How do I use FORCE FIELD ANALYSIS?

1. Explain the purpose of FORCE FIELD ANALYSIS. You might say, for example,

   We want to make sure that we are ready for both positive and negative responses to our suggestion for change. In order to prepare ourselves

SOURCE: Kurt Lewin, *Field Theory in Social Science* (Chicago: University of Chicago Press, 1951).

best, let's take a few minutes to analyze the forces that will likely support our idea, as well as the forces that likely will not. We can then look for actions to build on the forces that support us, and actions to diminish the arguments against the change.

2. <u>Draw a chart</u> or display a preprepared chart similar to the one in Fig. 7-10 and <u>ask your group to brainstorm the forces for and forces against the proposed idea or change.</u> Write the forces in the appropriate area of the chart.

   Note: If it is unclear whether a force is for or against the proposal, put it aside on another sheet for later analysis.

   Note: Leave enough space between the forces to write in strategies in the next step, and use different colored pens to differentiate the two.

Forces for (+)	Forces against (−)

Figure 7-10. FORCE FIELD ANALYSIS template.

3. After the lists are complete, <u>brainstorm actions to strengthen the forces for your proposed change and actions to weaken the opposition to that change.</u>

   Note: It may be helpful to ask yourselves some questions about each force to help you with your brainstorming. You might ask, for example, *"Who specifically is involved? What is the history of this force? How do we know that this force actually exists?"*

   Note: Spend the most time focusing on the strongest forces on each side.

4. After you have finished brainstorming, have your meeting group <u>select the most effective actions</u> to strengthen the forces for and diminish the forces against the proposal. Refer to Fig. 7-11 for a completed hypothetical example of a FORCE FIELD ANALYSIS chart.

   Note: Some solutions may address more than one 'force for' or 'force against.'

5. <u>Create action plans</u> as necessary. Plan how to incorporate these plans into your presentation to management, or next steps toward implementation.

Forces for (+)	Forces against (−)
Safety problems Document problems and costs *Down time* Document problems and costs *Improved productivity* Calculate productivity increases over time. When will equipment pay for itself?	*No budget* Show the cost benefits and time needed to recoup the money. *Skills training necessary—work flow disruption* Vendor chosen provides off-hours training, will not interrupt work flow. Employees willing to train off-hours.

Figure 7-11. Finished example of FORCE FIELD ANALYSIS chart.

8

7 Techniques to Implement Decisions

> 1. Smart Goals
>
> 2. Chart Actions
>
> 3. Goal Plan Go
>
> 4. Tree Chart
>
> 5. Call for Involvement
>
> 6. Test for Support
>
> 7. Individual Action Plan

Malcolm manages the mechanic shop of a freight shipping company.

Ideas and decisions come easy for us. But nothing ever seems to happen after we make our decisions. Our intentions are good but it seems that all our time goes to firefighting the crisis of the hour. Our customers are getting frustrated and some major accounts are talking about leaving. We need to move fast.

Meetings are more powerful and effective with an "implementation," "next steps," or "action" component. But while many groups agree on where they want to go and what they need to do, few plan how to get there. This often results in conflict, confusion, and diminished effectiveness. Gaining agreement on how these group decisions will be carried out strongly increases the likelihood of success.

The seven techniques described in this chapter demonstrate how to efficiently move a meeting group toward action. These techniques ensure agreement on actions, clarify roles and responsibilities, and formulate plans for review and follow-up. Techniques are:

- 63 SMART GOALS
- 64 CHART ACTIONS
- 65 GOAL PLAN GO
- 66 TREE CHART

- 67 CALL FOR INVOLVEMENT
- 68 TEST FOR SUPPORT
- 69 INDIVIDUAL ACTION PLANNING

63

SMART GOALS

> Specific
> Measurable
> Agreed upon
> Realistic
> Time bound

I think the goals we set are clear and agreed upon during our meetings, but even hours later there seems to be little agreement about exactly what we agreed to. How can we avoid this problem?

What is SMART GOALS?

SMART GOALS is a technique for obtaining clear agreement from your meeting group about exactly what is meant by any particular goal. This technique is also an excellent process for improving the likelihood that a specific goal will be implemented to the satisfaction of everyone who is involved.

The SMART in SMART GOALS is an acronym for Specific, Measurable, Agreed Upon, Realistic, and Time bound. The SMART GOALS technique requires that these five elements be included in the communication of every goal so that there will be understanding, agreement, commitment, and action on every level of the organization.

Often, broad organizational goals are set on a corporate level and then must be translated into more detailed operational goals as they cascade through the organization. These goals communicate what the priorities of an organization, group, or individual should be. SMART GOALS makes this process more manageable and trackable.

Following is a simple example of how SMART GOALS works and might cascade through an organization. The original corporate goal could be simple: *"Increase profits."* The SMART GOAL for the organization as a whole might then be written as: *"Increase our current profit margin of 5% to 15% by December 31, 1996."* As a result of this corporate goal, a SMART GOAL for a support service department of the organization might then be defined as: *"Decrease departmental operating costs by 10% by December 31, 1996."* Perhaps after the support service department has done some investigation on how to reach its goal, a specific area within that department might have a subsequent SMART GOAL: *"Decrease the cost of producing and distributing marketing materials by 25% by October 1, 1996."* And an individual within the department that produces and distributes marketing material may have an individual SMART GOAL: *"Create and lead a work team to identify methods to decrease the costs of producing and distributing marketing materials by 25% by October 1, 1996."*

To get the most from your SMART GOALS, you must proactively monitor the progress and results of each specific action plan designed to meet the originally defined goal.

There are serious consequences if this monitoring step doesn't occur. First, without effective follow-up, the specific actions included in your efforts may simply be forgotten. Second, a lack of sincere follow-up indicates a lack of seriousness about goal achievement. This speaks volumes to the people who work in the organization and it is unlikely that employees will follow through when actions are not tracked or rewarded. In both cases, the negative impact can be profound.

When do I use SMART GOALS?

- When you want to be sure that your goals are clear and easily tracked.
- When goals must cascade down through an organization.
- When performance of a group or individual must be measured and evaluated.

How do I use SMART GOALS?

1. After goals have been brainstormed and agreed upon, <u>introduce the SMART GOALS technique to your group.</u> In addition to explaining what makes a goal SMART, lead a brief discussion on the value of "smartening" goals. You might say, for example,

   In order to make sure that we all agree exactly on what each of these goals means, what our measurable targets are, and what time frames we must meet, let's take the time to make these goals SMART GOALS. SMART is an acronym that stands for specific, measurable, agreed upon, realistic and time bound.

   Write the acronym and its meanings on a chart like the one in Fig. 8-1.

   Then you might say, *"What do you see as advantages in having SMART GOALS?"*

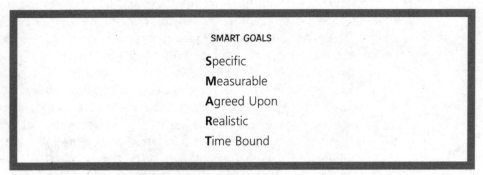

Figure 8-1. The SMART GOALS acronym.

2. Lead a discussion in which your meeting group <u>creates SMART GOALS</u> for each of the goals originally agreed upon.

   Option: When you have several goals and a large group, break the group into smaller groups, assign one or two goals to each small group, and ask them to report back on their drafted SMART GOALS to the larger group for approval. This saves time and increases the participation of everyone in the group. Use a chart similar to Fig. 8-2 to support this activity.

```
                    CREATE SMART GOALS

  1.  Pick a recorder and a timekeeper for your group.
                                                           1 minute

  2.  Smarten each goal by creating a short sentence or phrase which is:
      Specific
      Measurable
      Agreed Upon
      Realistic
      Time Bound
                                                    10 minutes per goal
  3.  Pick a spokesperson who will report back to the other participants.
                                                           1 minute
```

Figure 8-2. Instruction chart for SMART GOALS.

3. After all the SMART GOALS have been agreed upon by the group, <u>determine the best way to communicate the goals to others in the organization,</u> as well as when and how to monitor the progress of each SMART GOAL.

   Note: Instead of waiting to check results after the goal deadline, it's better to have logical checkpoints, especially for large and long-term SMART GOALS.

4. <u>Plan specific actions to reach your goals.</u>

   Option: See TREE CHART, Technique 66, to support these efforts.

   Note: As implementation begins, actions may need to be fine-tuned and priorities set in order to ensure that the most important actions to achieve the most critical goals take place.

64

CHART ACTIONS

We often agree to do things in our meetings, but forget exactly what the agreements were by the time the next meeting begins. We get in arguments about when things are supposed to be finished and who is supposed to do them. Is there a technique that can help us avoid these problems?

What is CHART ACTIONS?

CHART ACTIONS is a technique to document agreed upon actions as they are discussed in a meeting. This technique includes provisions for "Who will do What by When," and is an excellent way to move from vague action statements to specific action plans.

The CHART ACTIONS technique clarifies exactly what actions are agreed upon and when these actions will be accomplished. The process also identifies the people who are accountable, giving ownership to those who accept that responsibility, thus providing incentive that the actions will be fulfilled. These elements, when coupled with effective follow-through and monitoring, will contribute to the success of any action plan.

When do I use CHART ACTIONS?

■ Whenever your group is discussing issues that require action.

How do I use CHART ACTIONS?

1. When your meeting group will be discussing issues that require action, <u>create a chart labeled Actions or Next Steps</u> at the beginning of your meeting. Include three columns, headed What, Who, and By When (an example is illustrated in Fig. 8-3). Place the chart at a convenient spot in front of the room.

2. <u>As ideas for action come up during the meeting, write them down</u> in the What category. At that time, add both the Who and By When if they are clear. If the Who and By When are not clear, wait until the end of the meeting for clarification so as not to disrupt the flow of the meeting.

3. <u>As one of the last agenda items at the end of the meeting, go back to your chart.</u> Lead a discussion to confirm "Who will do What by When" for each action item displayed.

Actions		
What	Who	By When

Figure 8-3. CHART ACTIONS chart.

> *Note:* Sometimes there will be ideas that the group will not want to follow through on and sometimes issues will be tabled until a later meeting. Most issues, however, will require a further specific action.

> *Note:* Don't get bogged down. If an issue is controversial and you don't have time to discuss it during your meeting, make an agenda item to discuss this issue at a later date, such as at the next scheduled staff meeting.

4. <u>Follow up</u> as appropriate and necessary for each action item.

> *Note:* It is a good idea to go back to these lists of actions as one of your agenda items at the beginning of each meeting.

65

GOAL PLAN GO

*I recently read that there is a higher
likelihood that goals will be obtained
if the work to achieve those goals is started
immediately. I have a goal-setting meeting coming up
with a large group of people. After we set goals, I would like
to start some of the implementation planning as soon as possible. Is
there a technique that will help me do this?*

What is GOAL PLAN GO?

GOAL PLAN GO is a technique that invites your meeting participants to take responsibility for transforming the group's goals into action. The process allows individuals to choose which planning team they would like to join, and to have the first meeting of that planning team immediately.

Because enthusiasm and momentum are at their peak at the time that goals are defined and approved, the likelihood for effective implementation increases dramatically when the action planning can begin immediately. GOAL PLAN GO allows this process to take place.

When do I use GOAL PLAN GO?

- When you have a large meeting group that will be approving a number of goals.
- When it is difficult for the participants to meet together regularly.
- When your group has a history of good intentions but poor follow-through.

How do I use GOAL PLAN GO?

1. <u>Be sure that your meeting group has agreed upon a list of goals.</u> If you haven't already done so, write a list of these goals on a few pieces of chart paper with plenty of space between each of the goals. Display them around the room.

2. <u>Ask your participants to help create planning teams for each goal.</u> You might say, for example,

   We are going to take some time in today's meeting to plan how to turn our goals into action. To do that, we will create planning teams, one for each of our goals. Each planning team will be made up of a group of volunteers. Take a few minutes to think about which specific goal you would like to work on. Then write your name in the space under that goal. If you want or need to participate on the planning team for more than one goal, you can do so, but you must choose which one you will focus on

Figure 8-4. Instructions for creating action planning teams.

today. Write your name under each goal you are interested in, but place an asterisk after your name under all but the goal of primary interest. This will indicate that you are interested in being a part of that planning team, but will not be attending today's planning meeting.

Exhibit a chart similar to Fig. 8-4 to support your instructions.

3. <u>Designate an area in the room for each planning team to meet.</u>

4. <u>Give the groups guidelines</u> for their discussions and ask them to begin their planning processes. Refer to Fig. 8-5 for an example of these guidelines.

5. After an appropriate period of time (depending on the amount of time available in your meeting), <u>ask each group to report the results of its progress.</u> Have them include any agreed upon next steps or actions as well.

6. <u>Determine as a group how and when to monitor the progress of the implementation efforts.</u>

Figure 8-5. Planning team guidelines.

66

TREE CHART

We seem to have a difficult time moving from large, complex goals into detailed action plans. Is there a technique that can help us better organize our efforts in this type of situation?

What is TREE CHART?

TREE CHART is a technique for effectively detailing a complex action plan. After a goal has been agreed upon and approved, the next step is to create an action plan for achieving that goal. If the goal is large and complicated, the resulting action plan will have several levels and categories of activity.

TREE CHART is an extremely efficient technique for establishing the levels and categories of a complex action plan in a systematic and easy to understand form. Sometimes the details of a plan of this type will be completed on different levels and by different departments within an organization. TREE CHART serves this purpose well, and also provides an easy to follow process for visually tracking what actions will be done by whom and by when.

When do I use TREE CHART?

- When planning the details of how to reach a complex goal.
- When the actions for achieving a goal are multifaceted and multilayered.
- When you want to communicate and monitor what actions will happen where.

How do I use TREE CHART?

1. Review the SMART GOAL for which you are creating your action plan. (See SMART GOALS, Technique 63, for details.)

   Note: Be sure to include all the appropriate people in the meeting so that all levels, departments, and teams impacted by the goal and its actions are represented. If this is not possible, plan subsequent meetings to include all appropriate people.

2. Have your meeting group list the primary activities or categories of activities that will need to be accomplished in order for the goal to be reached. Chart their replies in TREE CHART form, which is little more than the visual form of a traditional outline. The structure of your TREE CHART will resemble the chart illustrated in Fig. 8-6.

   Note: Using sticky notes here allows your meeting group some flexibility. If the group doesn't like the way that the categorized information has been structured the first time around, the sticky notes can easily be moved around.

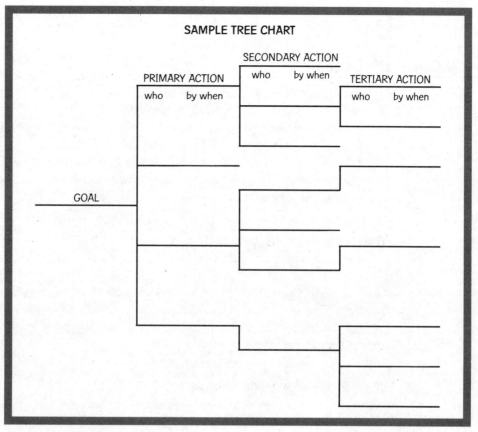

Figure 8-6. Sample TREE CHART.

3. Ask the group to <u>identify the next level of activities that will need to be accomplished,</u> charting their responses as noted in Step 2.

4. <u>Continue the process</u> as described in Steps 2 and 3 <u>to whatever level of detail is required and appropriate for the situation.</u>

   Note: This is usually to the point where small work teams and individuals are clear about the actions or next steps required from them.

5. <u>Add Who and By When information for every branch of your TREE CHART.</u>

   Note: When estimating time frames, work backwards from the goal. In other words, begin from the last required action in the process toward the first actions. By doing so, you are more likely to create time frames that meet the time commitment of the original goal.

6. <u>Review and complete your TREE CHART,</u> finalizing the format for formal reproduction.

7. <u>Plan the best way to monitor and follow up</u> on the implementation efforts.

67

CALL FOR INVOLVEMENT

Our group has difficulty determining specifically who should be involved in the implementation of our goals and even how they should be involved. Sometimes people want to participate but they're not included, and sometimes people are included when they really don't need or want to be. What do you suggest for avoiding this situation?

What is CALL FOR INVOLVEMENT?

CALL FOR INVOLVEMENT is a technique for establishing who will be involved in the implementation of a goal or project, and in what capacity.

The process gives individuals a choice between specific types and levels of involvement. The technique encourages participation, clarifies roles and responsibilities, and creates a stronger team for moving a goal or project from conception to successful implementation.

When do I use CALL FOR INVOLVEMENT?

- When it is difficult to determine who should be involved in a project or action plan, and at what level of involvement.
- When your meeting group has defined and approved a goal and is ready to plan its implementation.

How do I use CALL FOR INVOLVEMENT?

1. Summarize the projects or goals that your meeting group is focusing on.

   Note: Use charts or overheads to act as visual aids when appropriate.

2. Introduce the CALL FOR INVOLVEMENT technique, and briefly explain each of the categories of participation that will be used in the exercise. These categories are outlined in Fig. 8-7.

   Be sure to obtain agreement from your group on the validity of these categories of participation in your specific situation and modify the categories as appropriate and necessary.

3. Ask the participants to come forward and volunteer their names for the category or categories that they feel are appropriate for themselves.

> ### CALL FOR INVOLVEMENT
> #### Categories of Participation
>
> S   *(Sponsor)* I want to sponsor this activity/project.
>
> P   *(Planning)* I want to be involved in the preliminary planning.
>
> D   *(Doing)* I want to be part of making this happen.
>
> R   *(Research)* I have pertinent information to share during data collection.
>
> CC   *(CC: Memo)* I don't want to be involved but keep me informed.
>
> L   *(Later)* I might be interested but talk to me later.

Figure 8-7. CALL FOR INVOLVEMENT categories of participation.

Note: If there is more than one action, goal, or decision that is being implemented, ask your participants to write their names in the appropriate categories for each option.

Also invite participants to write in the names of other appropriate people they feel should be involved but are not present at the meeting. Create a chart, such as the one illustrated in Fig. 8-8, for this purpose.

4. When the group is finished signing up and all participants have returned to their seats, <u>debrief the results.</u> You might say, for example, *"What are your reactions? Do we have appropriate representation for each action to make this project work?"*

Note: If a goal or project has no sponsor it will very likely fail. In addition, if the majority of your meeting group want to be informed but do not have any enthusiasm or commitment for active involvement, the group needs to question the validity of the goal or project.

5. <u>Plan how the project will proceed and how to best monitor progress.</u> At this point you might ask, for example, *"What level of authority and responsibility will the working group have? How should we follow up? How will we measure success? Who will coordinate and communicate our efforts?"*

STATEMENT OF GOAL OR PROJECT

How do you choose to participate?

Write your name (and the names of any others not attending the meeting) in the category you would like or need to be involved in.

S	*(Sponsor)*
P	*(Planning)*
D	*(Doing)*
R	*(Research)*
CC	*(CC: Memo)*
L	*(Later)*

Figure 8-8. Instructions for CALL FOR INVOLVEMENT.

68

TEST FOR SUPPORT

Even when our group approves a decision for implementation, sometimes I get the feeling that there isn't total support for that decision. Is there a technique that would better ascertain true levels of support before we begin implementation?

What is TEST FOR SUPPORT?

TEST FOR SUPPORT is a technique that provides a process for discovering how much true support there is for a decision, goal, or action plan that has already been approved.

One cannot assume enthusiastic support from all group members simply because a decision has been approved by the group. This misguided assumption has been the downfall of many an implementation plan.

The TEST FOR SUPPORT technique involves people voting for their specific levels of support for a decision, goal, or action plan. Using this technique, a group can effectively measure this support and respond appropriately to secure the consensus required for successful implementation.

When do I use TEST FOR SUPPORT?

- When you want to clarify the true sentiments of meeting participants.
- When a decision or group of decisions has been made.
- When you feel you must have full support before moving forward.

How do I use TEST FOR SUPPORT?

1. <u>Introduce the TEST FOR SUPPORT technique and its purpose.</u> You might begin by saying, for example:

   Let's take a few minutes to discover the true level of support and enthusiasm we have for the decisions we have just made. Sometimes the approval of specific decisions is not enough. If we go forward with a false sense of enthusiasm about these decisions, their implementation will be very likely to fail.

2. <u>Explain how the technique works.</u> You might say, *"I am going to give each of you a piece of paper. Please write down your true sentiments about this decision."* Hand out a paper to each participant. Then you might say, for example, *"Based on the categories written on this chart, write down the number that best describes your position."* Display on an overhead or chart one of the two

TEST FOR SUPPORT

Write down the response that best describes your true feelings.

1 I support these actions.
2 I feel neutral about these actions.
3 I do not support these actions.
? I don't know.

Figure 8-9. Instructions for TEST FOR SUPPORT Option 1.

following options. Option 1 is illustrated in Fig. 8-9 and Option 2 is shown in Fig. 8-10.

3. Ask your participants to fold their papers when finished and pass them to the front.
4. Ask a participant near the front to read the scores while you note the number of votes on a prepared chart. Voting charts for Options 1 and 2 are shown in Figs. 8-11 and 8-12, respectively.
5. Debrief the results of the exercise. You might ask the group, for example, *"What are your reactions? Given this information, what changes are necessary to ensure success?"* Ask for information from the group as needed. You may need to ask, for example, *"What caused so many of you to be ambivalent? Why are you unwilling to spend the necessary time to make these decisions work?"*

TEST FOR SUPPORT

Write down the response that best describes your feelings.

4 I will do everything I possibly can to support these actions.
3 I agree with these actions and plan to put some time toward their success.
2 I agree but I'm not willing to do much.
1 I don't really care if it works or not.
0 I will smile and quietly sabotage these efforts.

Figure 8-10. Instructions for TEST FOR SUPPORT Option 2.

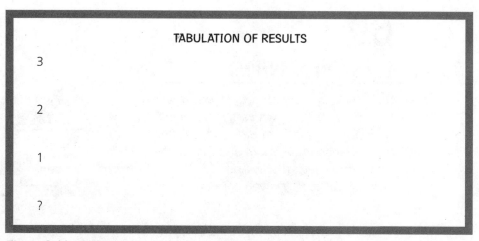

TABULATION OF RESULTS

3

2

1

?

Figure 8-11. Tabulation chart for TEST FOR SUPPORT Option 1.

6. Alter or further <u>examine your decisions if appropriate.</u> Postpone moving forward in your implementation planning until there is a high level of support and enthusiasm for the plan.

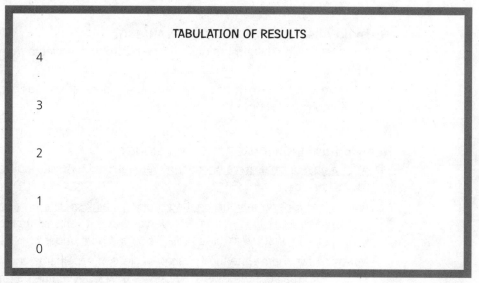

TABULATION OF RESULTS

4

3

2

1

0

Figure 8-12. Tabulation chart for TEST FOR SUPPORT Option 2.

69

INDIVIDUAL ACTION PLANNING

Sometimes I wish people would take responsibility for their own part in implementation. We have people from different areas of the organization in the room and I want them to simply say what they will do to help us achieve our overall goals. Do you have any suggestions?

What is INDIVIDUAL ACTION PLANNING?

INDIVIDUAL ACTION PLANNING is a simple technique for identifying individual commitments and contributions to the implementation of a goal.

The process involves each individual in the meeting group making a public statement of their intended actions to support the goal under consideration. This INDIVIDUAL ACTION PLAN communicates the specific commitments that each participant will undertake as a contribution to overall success.

When do I use INDIVIDUAL ACTION PLANNING?

- When the individual contributions to a goal can be completed independently of each other.
- When public commitment to a goal or action is a key to increasing the effectiveness of implementation.

How do I use INDIVIDUAL ACTION PLANNING?

1. <u>After a goal or goals have been identified,</u> introduce the INDIVIDUAL ACTION PLANNING technique.

2. <u>Ask the participants in your meeting group to think specifically about what they will do to support that goal.</u> Give everyone about ten minutes to write down his or her personal SMART GOALS relative to the goal under consideration.

   Note: Have them write their goals on a piece of paper large enough to be seen from across the room. (See SMART GOALS, Technique 63, for details.)

   Post an instruction chart similar to the one illustrated in Fig. 8-13 to support you during Steps 1 and 2.

3. <u>Ask each individual to stand up, one by one, to state his or her written commitments,</u> and place them on a prepared chart on the wall.

   Note: Unless you are a neutral facilitator, remember to participate in the exercise along with everybody else.

DEFINE YOUR PERSONAL ACTIONS TO ACHIEVE THIS GOAL

- Think about what specifically you can and will do to support this goal.
- Write down your personal contributions as a SMART GOAL or action. SMART stands for Specific, Measurable, Agreed upon, Realistic, and Time bound.
- Write this SMART GOAL on paper. Include your name. If you have more than one commitment, write SMART GOALS on separate pieces of paper.
- Be ready to communicate your commitments to the rest of the group.

10 minutes

Figure 8-13. Instruction chart for INDIVIDUAL ACTION PLANNING.

4. Debrief the individual statements of commitment. You might ask, for example, *What are your reactions to what you have heard from your colleagues? How satisfied are you with the level of commitment from yourself and others? How comfortable are you about the progress we will make if we all honor our commitments? What might get in the way of your group achieving what you have committed to? What should be done to eliminate those road blocks?*
5. Plan when and how to monitor progress.

9

3 Techniques to Evaluate Meeting Effectiveness

1. WHAT WENT WELL/ OPPORTUNITIES FOR IMPROVEMENT

2. TEAM EFFECTIVENESS CHART

3. WRITTEN QUESTIONS

Ralph's engineering meetings are good, but with a little help they could be even better.

> We evaluate the effectiveness of almost everything we do, but we never evaluate our meetings. I think some feedback would help us and I want to show that I'm willing to "walk the walk."

As with other products and services, meeting facilitators need feedback from their customers (in this case the participants) in order to continually increase their effectiveness. This chapter provides three techniques that give meeting facilitators specific processes to obtain accurate information about the effectiveness of their meetings. These techniques ask for different types of information in different ways, but all provide the meeting facilitator with the data necessary to accurately measure and consistently improve the quality of their meetings.

These three techniques are:

- 70 WHAT WENT WELL/OPPORTUNITIES FOR IMPROVEMENT
- 71 TEAM EFFECTIVENESS CHART
- 72 WRITTEN QUESTIONS

70

WHAT WENT WELL / OPPORTUNITIES FOR

IMPROVEMENT

I've been leading our team meetings now for almost a year but I've never asked for feedback on how I'm doing. Is there an accurate, fast, and easy way to get input from my group about how well our meetings are going?

What is WHAT WENT WELL / OPPORTUNITIES FOR IMPROVEMENT?

WHAT WENT WELL / OPPORTUNITIES FOR IMPROVEMENT is a technique for gathering feedback on how well your meetings work. This type of technique, sometimes called a process check, is usually scheduled at the end of a meeting, but it can be used at any time you feel it is necessary.

The primary focus of the WHAT WENT WELL / OPPORTUNITIES FOR IMPROVEMENT technique is to analyze the effectiveness of the processes and techniques that have been utilized in the specific meeting under consideration. This technique also gathers feedback on other aspects of the meeting, such as the quality of the content and results, participant behavior, and participation in general.

This type of feedback gives important information to the meeting facilitator. The information helps provide a basis for technique selection in subsequent meetings with the same meeting group, and also challenges the facilitator to work consistently to improve the product delivered.

When do I use WHAT WENT WELL / OPPORTUNITIES FOR IMPROVEMENT?

- When you want to receive honest feedback about the quality of your meetings.
- When you want to improve the caliber of your meetings.
- When you want meeting feedback to be open and shared by all.
- When you want meeting feedback to be formally quantified instead of informal.

How do I use WHAT WENT WELL / OPPORTUNITIES FOR IMPROVEMENT?

BEFORE THE MEETING

1. Put WHAT WENT WELL / OPPORTUNITIES FOR IMPROVEMENT on the meeting agenda.
2. Determine which option you want to use in your meeting. Variation 1 is designed to obtain verbal feedback from the whole meeting group, Variation 2 obtains this verbal information from small groups, and Variation 3 provides individual, written feedback. You may choose to use all of these variations

with the same meeting group over time to keep them from tiring of the same technique.

Note: You will need to allot between five and twenty minutes for this exercise, depending on the size of your meeting group and the specific technique option you choose to use. Variation 1 should require ten to fifteen minutes, Variation 2 about twenty minutes, and Variation 3 will take about five minutes.

3. Prepare two charts: one that looks similar to the one illustrated in Fig. 9-1, and the proper instruction chart for the technique option you will use (see Figs. 9-2 through 9-4).

Note: Some facilitators, when creating their WHAT WENT WELL / OPPORTUNITIES FOR IMPROVEMENT chart, write a "+" at the top of the What Went Well column and a "–" or "++" at the top of the Opportunities for Improvement column.

DURING THE MEETING

1. Introduce the WHAT WENT WELL / OPPORTUNITIES FOR IMPROVEMENT technique. If this is the first time your group has used this technique, take a minute to describe the purpose, process, and payoff of the exercise. (See 3P STATEMENTS, Technique 8, for more information.) You might say, for example,

The purpose of WHAT WENT WELL / OPPORTUNITIES FOR IMPROVEMENT is to hear from each of you how you feel our meeting went today. I'd like to hear both about what you thought went well, or was effective, and what you thought didn't go so well, where there are opportunities for improvement. Here's how we will do it.

+ *What Went Well*	++ *Opportunities for Improvement*

Figure 9-1. WHAT WENT WELL / OPPORTUNITIES FOR IMPROVEMENT chart.

Display and explain your prepared instructions from Variations 1, 2, or 3 outlined below. Then you might say, for example,

The payoff of this exercise hopefully will be a better meeting the next time we meet. I plan to incorporate your ideas, building on what went well, and look for ways to capitalize on our opportunities for improvement.

2. <u>Lead the exercise,</u> using one of the following three variations.

VARIATION 1. <u>Obtain verbal feedback as a full group.</u> This works well when your group is fewer than 20 participants and you have about ten to fifteen minutes at the end of your meeting.

a. Explain the exercise to the group, using a chart similar to the one shown in Fig. 9-2 as a visual aid. You might say,

In one or two brief sentences, tell us what you think went well and what you feel are our opportunities for improvement for this meeting.

b. Ask for a volunteer in the group to begin. Suggest the round-robin method (hearing from everyone in sequence) or popcorn method (members speak up whenever they want, no specific sequence is required or expected) for listening to everyone's comments.

c. Document all comments on your prepared chart.

d. Debrief the information, and obtain agreement on what can be done differently for the next meeting.

Note: Consider going through each item on the Opportunities for Improvement side of the chart to help the group identify specific actions for the next meeting.

Note: Make sure that the sound of your voice supports your openness to questions and concerns. If your voice doesn't support your words (due to sarcasm and defensiveness, for example) you will lose credibility.

WHAT WENT WELL / OPPORTUNITIES FOR IMPROVEMENT

Briefly, give us your feedback on today's meeting.

- What went well?
- What are our opportunities for improvement?

Let's hear from everyone; no passing, please.

Figure 9-2. Instruction chart for Variation 1.

VARIATION 2. <u>Obtain verbal feedback from small groups.</u> If your group includes more than 20 participants, break your group into a few small work groups. Be sure that each group has an easel, chart paper, and markers.

a. Explain the exercise to the groups, using a chart similar to Fig. 9-3 as a visual aid.

b. Give the groups five minutes to share and chart their feedback.

c. Ask each group for a 2-minute report back.

d. Debrief the information shared by each small group. To help the groups you might ask,

What are the commonalities? Which seem to be our strengths? Which areas should we concentrate on in order to make the greatest improvements?

WHAT WENT WELL / OPPORTUNITIES FOR IMPROVEMENT

- Pick a recorder and a reporter.
- Round-robin—no passing please.
- Briefly give your feedback on what went well and opportunities for improvement in today's meeting.

5 minutes

Figure 9-3. Instruction chart for Variation 2.

VARIATION 3. <u>Obtain individual, written feedback.</u> This option works well with small or large groups. Use it when you do not have or do not want to take time in the meeting for verbal feedback. The feedback can be reviewed at the next meeting or as part of the minutes of the meeting. This is an excellent feedback technique to use right before lunch in an all-day meeting, where corrections and modifications can then be made in the afternoon.

a. Explain the exercise, using a visual aid like the one shown in Fig. 9-4. Be sure that there are enough sticky notes within reach of all participants.

b. Begin the exercise. Place the prepared chart paper and easel by the door so that it is easy for participants to quickly stick their feedback on the chart as they leave the meeting.

c. After the participants have left, read and cluster the feedback. Decide what actions are appropriate given the feedback from the group. Decide how to incorporate their ideas and how to communicate your intentions, either as part of the minutes of the meeting, or at the beginning of the next meeting.

> **WHAT WENT WELL / OPPORTUNITIES FOR IMPROVEMENT**
>
> Please give us your feedback on today's meeting.
>
> - What went well?
> - What are our opportunities for improvement?
>
> Please write all ideas on sticky notes (one idea per sticky note).
> Stick your notes on the chart as you leave.

Figure 9-4. Instruction chart for Variation 3.

Note: If you use this option, give participants the results of the feedback when the meeting reconvenes, at the next meeting, or in the meeting minutes. It's best to cluster like comments together, so you can say, for example, *"Seven people made comments about the effectiveness of our brainstorming session"* before you read the comments verbatim. See CARD CLUSTERS, Technique 31, for details. Be sure not to sugarcoat the results or you will lose credibility. Consider stating your action plan for improvement based on these comments.

71

TEAM EFFECTIVENESS CHART

My team is very exacting and likes to use quantitative ratings. Is there a meeting evaluation technique I can use that satisfies these criteria?

What is TEAM EFFECTIVENESS CHART?

TEAM EFFECTIVENESS CHART is a technique that visually and quantifiably measures specific aspects of your meeting, such as level of open communication, satisfaction with results accomplished, how well the group honors the ideas of others, or other components of the meeting. The resulting measurements are charted on different grids with numerical rankings.

TEAM EFFECTIVENESS CHART incorporates MOVEMENT, Technique 16, and creates a chart that serves as a visual aid to display quantified group ratings. This chart can also be used as a benchmark for later evaluations.

When do I use TEAM EFFECTIVENESS CHART?

- When you want to get feedback on specific criteria.
- When you want feedback that is measurable.
- When you want to include everyone in nonverbal feedback.
- When you want to get feedback quickly about the quality of your meetings.

How do I use TEAM EFFECTIVENESS CHART?

BEFORE THE MEETING

1. Add TEAM EFFECTIVENESS CHART to the end of the meeting's agenda. Allow 15 minutes for rankings and a debriefing discussion.

2. Decide which components of your meeting are appropriate for the group to measure for effectiveness. You may want to consult with other meeting participants in determining these categories. Your group's ground rules (See GROUND RULES, Technique 3, for more information) will offer a springboard for ideas. Possible examples of these components include:
   - How well we listened to each other.
   - How well we stayed on track.
   - How satisfied we are with the results of our meeting.
   - How well we followed our ground rules.
   - How well we brainstormed creative ideas.

- How open and honest our communication was.
- How well we encouraged and accomplished full participation.
- How comfortable participants felt about speaking their minds.

3. Create charts similar to the two illustrated in Figs. 9-5 and 9-6.

    Note: If your meeting group is large, consider duplicating the information on two or three charts instead. This will avoid crowding when participants place their marks on the charts.

    Note: This process could also be done electronically.

DURING THE MEETING

1. Introduce the TEAM EFFECTIVENESS CHART technique. If this is the first time your group is using this technique, explain what it is used for and how to use it. You might say, for example,

    TEAM EFFECTIVENESS CHART is a technique for visually measuring your feedback about our meeting. These measurements will allow us to look at our strengths and weaknesses as a meeting group. We can then look for methods to improve our effectiveness in our upcoming meetings. We can also use these measurements as a benchmark. After we work to improve, we can measure ourselves again and see what progress we have made.

    Share the measurements you will be employing, using your charts to support you. Explain how and why the components to be measured were chosen.

2. Ask participants to come forward and mark how well they think the team did in each category under consideration. They should indicate their ratings by putting a large dot on the chart in the appropriate place. You may provide sticky dots or markers for this exercise.

PLOT YOUR RESPONSE							
5 (High)							
4							
3							
2							
1 (Low)							
	A	B	C	D	E	F	G

Figure 9-5. TEAM EFFECTIVENESS CHART.

```
                                    KEY

    A   How well did we listen to each other?

    B   How well did we stay on track?

    C   How satisfied are you with our meeting results?

    D   How well did we follow our ground rules?

    E   How well did we brainstorm creative ideas?

    F   How open and honest was our communication?

    G   How well did we encourage and accomplish full participation?
```

Figure 9-6. TEAM EFFECTIVENESS CHART questions key.

3. After everyone has finished and is seated, <u>debrief the information as a group.</u> Here are some sample questions that may be appropriate.

   As you look at our chart, what stands out for you? What conclusions can we draw from this information? What are we particularly good at? What would you say are our major opportunities for improvement? What should we target as actions for improving our meetings? How should we accomplish these actions?

   Chart the group's responses and create a list of action items based on the major opportunities for improvement.

4. After the meeting, <u>keep the charts your team has developed.</u> Be sure to write the date on each of them.

5. <u>Benchmark your group's progress</u> in the next meeting or in whichever future meeting you and your group feel is appropriate. Compare your progress against the first measurement.

   a. Repeat Steps 1 and 2 but on a new chart.

   b. To debrief, bring out the old chart, and place it next to its counterpart from today's meeting.

   c. As a group, measure numerically the difference between your previous rankings and this meeting's rankings.

   d. Use or modify the debriefing questions in Step 3. Create a new action plan as necessary. You might also consider bringing out your old action plan to see if you have accomplished those actions yet.

   e. Keep the charts or a summary of the charts for benchmarking in the future.

72

WRITTEN QUESTIONS

In addition to meeting together, sometimes our group meets by phone or across locations and even via E-mail. Is there a meeting evaluation technique that I can use both inside and outside a face-to-face meeting?

What is WRITTEN QUESTIONS?

WRITTEN QUESTIONS is a technique for gathering written feedback on your meeting's effectiveness from each individual in the meeting. The technique involves each participant's completing a preprepared meeting evaluation questionnaire.

WRITTEN QUESTIONS, like the other meeting evaluation techniques described in this book, does more than simply analyze and measure the effectiveness of your meetings. Like a good antivirus program for your computer, these techniques expose problem areas in your meetings and also provide the insights to correct those problems and weaknesses. Their importance to meeting success and their recommended consistent use, therefore, cannot be overemphasized.

When do I use WRITTEN QUESTIONS?

- When you don't have time to evaluate the meeting as a group.
- When there are participants in different locations.
- When you want to use an alternative to verbal feedback in your meeting.

How do I use WRITTEN QUESTIONS?

BEFORE THE MEETING

1. Reserve a few minutes near the end of your meeting agenda for the WRITTEN QUESTIONS evaluation technique.

2. Prepare the WRITTEN QUESTIONS that you would like to use in your meeting. Two example questionnaires are illustrated in Figs. 9-7 and 9-8.

   Using one of these two templates, create a questionnaire that meets the specific needs of your meeting group.

   Note: When creating your questionnaire, be sure to ask OPEN-ENDED QUESTIONS (see Technique 34 for details).

DURING THE MEETING

1. Near the conclusion of your meeting, introduce the WRITTEN QUESTIONS technique and review the instructions and contents of your questionnaire.

MEETING QUESTIONNAIRE

As you reflect back on our meeting, what are your thoughts?

How effective was this meeting for you? Please circle one:

1   Very effective

2   Somewhat effective

3   Somewhat ineffective

4   Very ineffective

Why?

What do you think we did well?

What would you suggest we do differently next time?

What additional comments do you have?

Figure 9-7. Meeting questionnaire Variation A.

MEETING QUESTIONNAIRE

On a scale of 1-10 (1=very poor, 10=excellent), how would you rate your satisfaction with our meeting's results?

1———2———3———4———5———6———7———8———9———10

On a scale of 1-10, how would you rate our use of your time?

1———2———3———4———5———6———7———8———9———10

Comments.

Figure 9-8. Meeting questionnaire Variation B.

Note: It is best to schedule the meeting evaluation as the second to the last agenda item. End the meeting with another short agenda item, such as "plan the next meeting." If you ask people to complete a meeting evaluation questionnaire as you are about to dismiss the meeting, only a few people will stay to do so or will take the time required to make it a meaningful exercise. Including a short agenda item afterward will ensure that everyone will take the time to complete the questionnaire.

2. <u>Ask your participants to complete the questionnaire and return it to you</u> as they leave the meeting.

Option A: Use the format shown in Fig. 9-8 as a chart instead of an individual questionnaire. Place this chart near the door at the end of your meeting, so your participants can rate each question as they leave the meeting. Be sure to provide sticky notes so they can write and post their comments as well.

Option B: When your group is meeting electronically and won't be meeting face-to-face, send your chosen questionnaire to each participant before the meeting begins. Ask them to complete and return the material by fax or E-mail immediately after the meeting.

AFTER THE MEETING

<u>Collect, compile, and communicate the data received from your WRITTEN QUESTIONS.</u>

Note: In addition to providing the information generated from the questionnaire, be sure to communicate your intended actions as a result of the feedback.

Index

Agendas, 11-13, 24-26
  creation, 18-19
  examples, 12, 14-15, 20-22
  facilitator's version, 18-19
  order, 18
  participant's version, 18-19
  premeeting planning questions, 13, 16-18
  template, 19
Alternatives, to meeting, 25-26
Analogies and Metaphors, 57-59
Art, 55-56
Assertiveness, 7
Atmosphere, 23
Attributes:
  successful individual, 6-7
    assertiveness, 7
    confidence and enthusiasm, 8
    creativity, 7
    dedicated to learning, 8
    flexibility, 7-8
    good sense of humor, 7
    high self-esteem, 8
    intuition, 7
    sincerity, 8

Attributes (*Cont.*)
    team player, 8
  successful participant, 8-9

Bell, 44
Beverages and food, 23
Boeing Commercial Airplane Group, 78
Breaking a Stalemate, 105-106
Breaks, 60-61
Brainstorming, 89
  Breaking a Stalemate, 105-106
  Card Clusters, 99-101
  Mindmapping, 92-96
  Story Boarding, 97-98
  STP (Situation, Target, Proposal), 102-104
  The Old-Fashioned Way, 90-91
Buzan, Tony, 92

Call for Involvement, 194-196
Change in meeting style, 25
Chart Actions, 188-189
Charting, 53-54

Checklists:
  is this book for me? 3
  premeeting planning questions, 13, 16-18
Clearing, 31-33
Confidence, 8
Content Experts, 139-141
Continual improvement, 25
Creativity, 7
  boosting, 73
  techniques for increasing creativity and teamwork:
    Incrediballs, 78-80
    Milestones, 85-86
    New Glasses, 76-77
    Team Learning, 81-82
    The Funeral, 87-88
    Thinking Out of the Box, 74-75
    Two Truths and a Lie, 83-84
Criteria Matrix, 173-178

Daniels, William, 173
Debecq, A. L., 133
Decisions:
  implementing, introduction to, 184
  making, introduction to, 157
  techniques for implementing decisions:
    Call for Involvement, 194-196
    Chart Actions, 188-189
    Goal Plan Go, 190-191
    Individual Action Planning, 200-201
    Smart Goals, 185-187
    Test for Support, 197-199
    Tree Chart, 192-193
  techniques for making decisions:
    Criteria Matrix, 173-178
    Dots, 164-165
    Force Field Analysis, 181-183
    Idea Swap, 171-172
    Impact and Changeability Analysis, 179-180
    Multivoting, 160-161
    Negative Voting, 162-163
    Nominal Prioritization, 168-169
    100 Votes, 166-167
    3 For/3 Against, 170
    Vroom Yetton Decision-Making Model, 158-159
Dedication to learning, 8
Delphi Technique, 119-120
Delta Point, 102
Documentation, 18
  meeting minutes, 24
Dots, 164-165

Enthusiasm, 8

Environment:
  meeting, 19-20
  preparation, 19-20
    atmosphere, 23
    food and beverages, 23
    interruptions, 24
    room arrangement, 23
    setting the stage, 24
    temperature, 23
    windows, 20
Evaluating:
  meeting effectiveness, 202
  techniques for evaluating meeting effectiveness:
    Team Effectiveness Chart, 208-210
    What Went Well/Opportunities for Improvement, 203-207
    Written Questions, 211-213
Expectations Survey, 121-123

Facilitator, effective, attributes of, 6-8
5 Whys, 151
Flexibility, 7-8, 26
Flowcharting, Process Flow Charting, 135-138
Focus Groups, 113-115
Food and beverages, 23
Force Field Analysis, 181-183
Fosmire, Fred, 102
Funeral, 87-88

Goal setting, techniques for:
  Goal Plan Go, 190-191
  SMART Goals, 185-187
Go/No Go, 52
Ground Rules, 34-36

Handouts, 17
How to use this book, 4-5
  develop your own techniques, 4-5
  skim the book, 4
  toolbox, 4

Ideas, 89
  brainstorming techniques:
    Breaking a Stalemate, 105-106
    Card Clusters, 99-101
    Mindmapping, 92-96
    Story Boarding, 97-98
    STP (Situation, Target, Proposal), 102-104
    The Old-Fashioned Way, 90-91
  Idea Swap, 171-172
Impact and Changeability Analysis, 179-180

Implementing decisions, 184
   Call for Involvement, 194-196
   Chart Actions, 188-189
   Goal Plan Go, 190-191
   Individual Action Planning, 200-201
   Smart Goals, 185-187
   Test for Support, 197-199
   Tree Chart, 192-193
Incrediballs, 78-80
Individual:
   styles, 5-6
   techniques:
      Individual Action Planning, 200-201
      Individual Interviews, 110-112
Information:
   gathering, introduction to, 107
   gathering techniques:
      Content Experts, 139-141
      Delphi Technique, 119-120
      Expectations Survey, 121-123
      5 Whys, 151
      Focus Groups, 113-115
      Individual Interviews, 110-112
      Is/Not Is, 131-132
      Keep/Throw, 145-146
      New Shoes, 149-150
      Nominal Group Process, 133-134
      Open-Ended Questions, 108-109
      Passing Notes, 124-127
      Process Flowcharting, 135-138
      Prouds and Sorries, 142-144
      Questionnaires, 116-118
      Skits, 128-130
      SWOTs, 152-156
      Working Break, 147-148
Interruptions, limiting, 24
Interviews:
   verbal techniques:
      Focus Groups, 113-115
      Individual Interviews, 110-112
   written techniques:
      Delphi Technique, 119-120
      Questionnaires, 116-118
Introductions, 29-30
Intuition, 7
Is/Is Not, 131-132

Keep/Throw, 145-146
Kepner, Charles H., 131

Leader's guide, 18
Lewin, Kurt, 181

Meetings:
   alternatives, 25-26
   changing, 2, 25-26
   environment, 19-20
      atmosphere, 23
      food and beverages, 23
      interruptions, 24
      room arrangement, 23
      setting the stage, 24
      temperature, 23
      windows, 20
   evolution of, 2-3
   flexibility, 26
   history of, 2-3
   logistics, 17
   minutes, 24
   participants, 8-9, 13
   planning, 11-13
   premeeting planning questions, 13, 16-18
      agenda item questions, 16-17
      cornerstone questions, 13, 16
      logistical questions, 17
      reporting questions, 18
   success, 8-9, 24-26
Milestones, 85-86
Mindmapping, 92-96
Minutes of meeting, 24
Movement, 62-63
Multivoting, 160-161
Music, 66-67

Negative Voting, 162-163
New Glasses, 76-77
New Shoes, 149-150
Nominal Group Process, 133-134
Nominal Prioritization, 168-169

Ohmae, Kenichi, 105
100 Votes, 166-167
Open-Ended Questions, 108-109
Osborn, A. F., 90
Overheads, 17

Participation:
   agenda planning, 16-19, 24-26
   history of, 2-3
   meeting, 2-3
   philosophy of , 1-3
   why use, 2-3
Passing Notes, 124-127
Personal styles, 5-6

Planning, 24-26
   agendas, 12-13, 18-19
      samples, 12, 14-15, 20-22
      template, 19
   meetings, 11-13
   premeeting planning questions, 13, 16-18
Presentation:
   flexibility, 25
   planning, 16
Productivity:
   improving, 27-28
   techniques:
      for defining and controlling meeting behavior:
         Clearing, 31-33
         Ground Rules, 34-36
         Introductions, 29-30
         Pulse Check, 37-39
      for improving the clarity of communication:
         Analogies and Metaphors, 57-59
         Art, 55-56
         Charting, 53-54
      for keeping the energy high:
         Breaks, 60-61
         Movement, 62-63
         Music, 66-67
         Toys, 64-65
      for keeping your meetings on track:
         Go/No Go, 52
         Self-Management, 50-51
         Shredded Questions, 47-49
         The Bell, 44
         3P Statements, 45-46
         Unfinished Business, 40-41
         Verbal Warnings, 42-43
      for increasing participation:
         Small Groups, 70-72
         Writing, 68-69
Prouds and Sorries, 142-144
Pulse Check, 37-39

Questionnaires, 116-118

Recording of meeting minutes, 24
Reporting of meeting minutes, 24
Room:
   arrangement, 23
   atmosphere, 23
   seating options, 23
   setting the stage, 24
   temperature, 23

Seating options, 23
Self-esteem, 8
Setting the stage, 24

Skits, 128-130
STP (Situation, Target, Proposal), 102-104
Self-Management, 50-51
Sense of humor, 7
Shredded Questions, 47-49
Sincerity, 8
Small Groups, 70-72
SMART Goals, 185-187
Spain, Caryn, 121, 173
SWOTs (Strengths, Weaknesses Opportunities and
    Threats), 152-156
Styles, individual and personal, 5-6
Story Boarding, 97-98

Team Effectiveness Chart, 208-210
Team Learning, 81-82
Team player, 8-9
Teamwork:
   Incrediballs, 78-80
   Milestones, 85-86
   New Glasses, 76-77
   Team Learning, 81-82
   The Funeral, 87-88
   Thinking Out of the Box, 74-75
   Two Truths and a Lie, 83-84
Techniques:
   for boosting creativity and teamwork:
      Incrediballs, 78-80
      Milestones, 85-86
      New Glasses, 76-77
      Team Learning, 81-82
      The Funeral, 87-88
      Thinking Out of the Box, 74-75
      Two Truths and a Lie, 83-84
   for brainstorming ideas:
      Breaking a Stalemate, 105-106
      Card Clusters, 99-101
      Mindmapping, 92-96
      Story Boarding, 97-98
      STP (Situation, Target, Proposal), 102-104
      The Old-Fashioned Way, 90-91
   for evaluating meeting effectiveness:
      Team Effectiveness Chart, 208-210
      What Went Well/Opportunities for Improve-
        ment, 203-207
      Written Questions, 211-213
   for gathering information:
      Content Experts, 139-141
      Delphi Technique, 119-120
      Expectations Survey, 121-123
      5 Whys, 151
      Focus Groups, 113-115
      Individual Interviews, 110-112

Techniques, for gathering information (*Cont.*)
    Is/Not Is, 131-132
    Keep/Throw, 145-146
    New Shoes, 149-150
    Nominal Group Process, 133-134
    Open-Ended Questions, 108-109
    Passing Notes, 124-127
    Process Flowcharting, 135-138
    Prouds and Sorries, 142-144
    Questionnaires, 116-118
    Skits, 128-130
    SWOTs, 152-156
    Working Break, 147-148
  for implementing decisions:
    Call for Involvement, 194-196
    Chart Actions, 188-189
    Goal Plan Go, 190-191
    Individual Action Planning, 200-201
    Smart Goals, 185-187
    Test for Support, 197-199
    Tree Chart, 192-193
  for improving meeting productivity:
    defining and controlling meeting behavior:
      Clearing, 31-33
      Ground Rules, 34-36
      Introductions, 29-30
      Pulse Check, 37-39
    improving the clarity of communication:
      Analogies and Metaphors, 57-59
      Art, 55-56
      Charting, 53-54
    keeping the energy high:
      Breaks, 60-61
      Movement, 62-63
      Music, 66-67
      Toys, 64-65
    keeping your meetings on track:
      Go/No Go, 52
      Self-Management, 50-51
      Shredded Questions, 47-49
      The Bell, 44
      3P Statements, 45-46
      Unfinished Business, 40-41
      Verbal Warnings, 42-43

Techniques, for improving meeting productivity (*Cont.*)
  increasing participation:
    Small Groups, 70-72
    Writing, 68-69
  for making decisions:
    Criteria Matrix, 173-178
    Dots, 164-165
    Force Field Analysis, 181-183
    Idea Swap, 171-172
    Impact and Changeability Analysis, 179-180
    Multivoting, 160-161
    Negative Voting, 162-163
    Nominal Prioritization, 168-169
    100 Votes, 166-167
    3 For/3 Against, 170-171
    Vroom Yetton Decision-Making Model, 158-159
Temperature, 23
Test for Support, 197-199
Thinking Out of the Box, 74-75
3 For/3 Against, 170
3P Statements, 45-46
Time frames, estimating for agenda, 17, 26
Tragoe, Benjamin B., 131
Tree Chart, 192-193
Toys, 64-65
Two Truths and a Lie, 83-84

Unfinished Business, 40-41

Van de Ven, A. H., 133
Verbal Warnings, 42-43
Visual aids, 17
Vroom, Victor, 158
Vroom Yetton Decision-Making Model, 158-159

Weisbord, Marvin, 142, 145
What Went Well/Opportunities for Improvement,
    203-207
Working Break, 147-148
Writing, 68-69
Written Questions, 211-213

Yetton, Philip, 158

About the Author

Ava S. Butler is a trainer and senior consultant with Gemini Consulting in London. A specialist in organizational development and meeting strategy, her international client list includes Microsoft, US West, and Boeing.